The Azar Grammar Series

TEST BANK for

UNDERSTANDING AND USING

ENGLISH GRAMMAR

Third Edition

Mark Wade Lieu

Longman

Test Bank for Understanding and Using English Grammar
Third Edition

Pearson Education, 10 Bank Street, White Plains, NY 10606

Vice president, director of publishing: Allen Ascher
Editorial director: Louisa Hellegers
Senior development manager: Penny Laporte
Development editor: Janet Johnston
Vice president, director of design and production: Rhea Banker
Associate director of electronic production: Aliza Greenblatt
Executive managing editor: Linda Moser
Production manager: Ray Keating
Production editor: Robert Ruvo
Senior manufacturing buyer: Dave Dickey
Cover design adaptation: Pat Wosczyk
Text composition: Rainbow Graphics

ISBN: 0-13-958695-4

3 4 5 6 7 8 9 10-BAH-10 09 08 07

Contents

Introduction

This Test Bank was developed to accompany *Understanding and Using English Grammar, Third Edition*. For each chapter, there are short quizzes of five to a dozen items for a related group of grammatical points. The quizzes are designed to be completed in approximately ten minutes, permitting the teacher to use the quizzes to do quick checks of student understanding and to use what has been taught. Each chapter ends with a comprehensive chapter test. The formats of the questions in the chapter tests follow those used in previous quizzes. In this way, students are prepared for the format of the chapter test as well as for its content. Also included are a midterm exam and a final exam that can be used in conjunction with the other tests and quizzes or separately.

The quizzes, tests, and exams are formatted for easy duplication. Each set of items is accompanied by specific directions. Permission is granted to duplicate as many copies as needed for classroom use only.

Great care has been taken to provide valid and appropriate items in all tests and quizzes. Students will encounter a variety of test formats, from closed formats such as multiple choice to more open formats such as sentence writing and completion and error identification. The answer key provides definitive answers where possible and examples of acceptable answers where a variety of responses are possible.

CHAPTER 1
Overview of Verb Tenses

■ **Quiz 1:** The simple and progressive tenses.

Answer the questions.

1. What is one thing you do every day between 6 P.M. and 9 P.M.?
   _____*I watch the evening news on TV.*_____

2. When does your English class meet?
   _____

   _____

3. What did you do last night after you ate dinner?
   _____

   _____

4. What are you going to do this weekend?
   _____

   _____

5. What movie is playing at a local movie theater?
   _____

   _____

6. When you fell asleep last night, what were you thinking about?
   _____

   _____

■ **Quiz 2:**   The perfect, future, and perfect progressive tenses.

    A. Put the words in the correct order to form a clear sentence.

      1. a. *(John, his English, 6:00 P.M., has been studying, since)*

          <u>John has been studying his English since 6:00 P.M.</u>

        b. *(Mary, her English, 6:00 P.M., studied, at)*

          _____

      2. a. *(John, in New York, five years, has lived, for)*

          _____

        b. *(Mary, in New York, five years, has been living, for)*

          _____

      3. a. *(Mary, dinner, the party, will have eaten, before, begins)*

          _____

        b. *(John, dinner, the party, will eat, before, begins)*

          _____

    B. Look at each pair of sentences in **A.** If the meaning of the two sentences is the same, write ***the same***. If the meaning is different, explain what the difference is.

      1.   <u>*In a, John is still studying. In b, Mary is finished.*</u>

      2. _____

      3. _____

■ **Quiz 3:** Spelling of *-ing* and *-ed* forms.

Complete the sentences with either the ***-ing*** or the ***-ed*** form of the verb in parentheses.

1. *(tie)* Tina _____*tied*_____ a ribbon in her hair before she went to the party.

2. *(ask)* Mrs. Tom was _____ about your new job.

3. *(prefer)* Philip _____ taking the bus to driving to work.

4. *(listen)* John can't hear you because he is _____ to his stereo.

5. *(study)* Barbara has been _____ French for several years.

6. *(sit)* All the students are _____ quietly and are ready for the test.

7. *(lie)* Daniel was _____ down because he felt tired.

8. *(destroy)* The strong earthquake _____ many houses.

9. *(trim)* Karen _____ her sister's hair in the kitchen.

10. *(open)* A new bookstore is _____ next to the meat market.

11. *(train)* My supervisor was _____ two new workers yesterday.

■ CHAPTER 1 TEST

A. Put the words in the correct order to form a correct sentence.

1. a. *(Mary, Italian food, has eaten)*

   _____

   b. *(John, Italian food, ate, last night)*

   _____

2. a. *(John, in his garden, for over an hour, worked)*

   _____

   b. *(Mary, in her garden, for over an hour, has been working)*

   _____

3. a. *(John, his mother, is going to visit, next week)*

   _____

   b. *(Mary, her mother, is visiting, next week)*

   _____

4. a. *(Mary, her bicycle, for exercise, at 7, in the morning, rides)*

   _____

   b. *(John, his bicycle, for exercise, is riding)*

   _____

5. a. *(Mary, her homework, she, to bed, before, will have finished, goes)*

   _____

   b. *(John, his homework, he, to bed, before, will finish, goes)*

   _____

B. For each pair of sentences in **A**, if the meaning of the two sentences is the same, write *the same*. If the meaning is different, explain what the difference is.

1. ___*In a,*_____

2. _____

3. _____

4. _____

5. _____

CHAPTER 2
Present and Past,
Simple and Progressive

■ **Quiz 1:** Simple present vs. present progressive.

A. Write one sentence to tell what each person does.

1. Fireman _____*A fireman puts out fires.* OR *A fireman saves lives.*_____

2. Waitress _____

_____

3. Teacher _____

_____

4. Businesswoman _____

_____

5. Pilot _____

_____

6. Secretary _____

_____

B. Pretend that you are standing in the middle of a shopping mall. What do you see? Write five sentences.

_____*A woman is carrying three shopping bags.*_____

_____

_____

_____

_____

_____

■ **Quiz 2:** Stative verbs and *be* + adjective.

    A. Complete the sentences, using present verbs of the words in parentheses. Choose between a stative and a progressive meaning.

     1. This soup *(taste)* _____*tastes*_____ too spicy.

     2. Martha is in the kitchen. She *(taste)* _____ the soup before she serves it.

     3. That movie *(appear)* _____ very popular. There are a lot of people in line.

     4. The butcher *(weigh)* _____ the beef for his customer.

     5. He is *(see)* _____ the doctor right now.

     6. She *(see)* _____ very well and doesn't need glasses.

     7. I *(feel, not)* _____ very well today. I may go home early.

     8. Her bad behavior *(surprise)* _____ me.

     9. He *(appreciate)* _____ all the help you have given him.

    10. Martin *(feel)* _____ the pressure of his new job.

    B. Complete each sentence with an adjective.

     1. That man likes to hurt cats and dogs. He is very _____*cruel*_____.

     2. This math problem doesn't make sense. It is _____.

     3. She always says, "Thank you" and "Excuse me." She is very

       _____.

     4. What is that _____ smell? It smells like rotten eggs.

     5. I couldn't go to sleep because the television program was so

       _____.

     6. He always forces his way into line and never waits his turn. He is very

       _____.

7. The teacher gave us both the same grade, but I got more points than he did. That's _____.

8. During a test, you must not talk or make other noise. Everyone should be

   _____.

9. My roommate is useless. He never does any work. He just lies on the sofa and watches TV. He's _____.

10. The last time I ate was last night. It's already noon. I'm very _____.

11. My son never takes care of his possessions. He is very _____.

■ **Quiz 3:** Irregular past tense verbs.

Answer the questions. Begin each answer with **"Yes, he ... "**

1. It's almost dinner time. Did John set the table? _____ *Yes, he set the table.* _____

2. Did John lay the papers on the hall table? _____

   _____

3. John didn't bring a jacket. Did he freeze outside today? _____

   _____

4. Did John swim in the 1,000-meter race? _____

   _____

5. John isn't feeling well. Did he lie down for awhile? _____

   _____

6. Did John sweep the floor this morning? _____

   _____

7. Did John pay you for the goblet that he broke? _____

   _____

▪ **Quiz 4: Simple past vs. past progressive.**

Complete the sentences, using the simple past or the past progressive.

1. Mary was chopping some vegetables when she *(cut)* _____*cut*_____ her finger with the knife.

2. When Mary cut her finger, it *(begin)* _____ to bleed.

3. While Mary *(work)* _____ on her homework, she was listening to the television.

4. When Mary *(finish)* _____ the newspaper, she washed the breakfast dishes.

5. When Mary stopped smoking, she *(begin)* _____ to eat candy all the time.

6. While Mary was pruning the rose bush, she *(hurt)* _____ her finger on a thorn.

7. While Mary *(ride)* _____ the train, she worked on her report.

8. When Mary woke up, she *(make)* _____ a cup of coffee for herself.

9. When Mary went to Los Angeles, she *(go)* _____ to Disneyland every day.

10. When Mary *(drop)* _____ her laptop computer, she started to cry.

11. While Mary *(shop)* _____ for a new computer, she ran into an old friend.

■ **Quiz 5:** Using progressive verbs with *always* to complain; using progressive verbs with expressions of place.

A. Someone you know has many bad habits. These bad habits annoy you. Pretend you are complaining to a friend about this person. Write five sentences about the person's bad habits. Use **always**, **constantly**, or **forever**.

1. _____*My roommate is always leaving dirty laundry on the floor.*_____

2. _____

3. _____

4. _____

5. _____

6. _____

B. Answer the questions, using the present progressive or the past progressive. Use the expression of place in parentheses and add your own words.

1. **A:** Where is Sally? *(in the garden)*

   B: _____*She is in the garden trimming the bushes.*_____

2. **A:** John didn't come home until late. Where was he? *(at a night club)*

   B: _____

3. **A:** Is Tom at home? *(at the supermarket)*

   B: No. _____

4. **A:** Where is Marian? *(on an airplane)*

   B: _____

5. **A:** Were you home last weekend? *(at my grandmother's)*

   B: No. _____

6. **A:** What are you doing? *(in the classroom)*

   B: _____

■ CHAPTER 2 TEST

A. For each situation, write a sentence using **when** or **while**.

1. A man is inside his car on the side of the freeway. On his face is a look of dismay. Through the windshield, we can see that his gas gauge is on EMPTY.

    _____*While the man was driving, his car ran out of gas.*_____ OR _____

    _____*When the man ran out of gas, he was driving on a freeway.*_____

2. A woman is walking down the street. She is wearing earphones connected to a portable cassette player. We can hear the music from her earphones.

    _____

    _____

3. A young girl is setting the table for dinner. A broken glass is on the floor. She seems to be distressed.

    _____

    _____

4. The whole family is at home. Two children are at a table doing homework. Their father is sitting in the living room, reading a newspaper. Their mother is sitting in an armchair, reading a book.

    _____

    _____

5. A young boy is sitting on the ground crying. Next to him is his bicycle. The front wheel is bent. Next to the boy is a STOP sign. There is a large dent in the STOP sign pole.

    _____

    _____

6. A man is in a park next to a bush covered with flowers. In his hand is a single flower. There is a red welt on his face. He is waving his hands around, trying to chase away some bees.

    _____

    _____

B. Complete each sentence with an appropriate word or words.

1. I can't believe it. You just ate lunch. Are you really ____*hungry*____ again so soon?

2. You can't talk to Mr. James right now because he _____ another student.

3. Brian cannot study in this room because it is too _____.

4. If you don't feel well, maybe you should _____ down for a while.

5. Karen is very _____ and always gives her seat on the bus to older people.

6. Steven is in the library _____ a book.

7. I didn't know about the party for me at all. It really _____ me.

8. I was very tired yesterday, but after a good night's sleep, today I _____ full of energy.

9. The workers were very _____ and forgot to lock the door when they left for the day.

10. The little boy _____ another toy because he broke the first one.

CHAPTER 3
Perfect and Perfect Progressive Tenses

■ **Quiz 1:** Present perfect vs. simple past.

Combine each pair of sentences, using *after, since,* or *while.*

1. *first:* Sally will take her daughter to child care.
   later: She will go to work.

   _____Sally will go to work after she takes her daughter to child care._____

2. *first:* Patty was watching TV.
   next: Her mother told her to come to dinner.

   _____

   _____

3. *first:* Sally lied to her friend Jane.
   next: Jane has not spoken to Sally.

   _____

   _____

4. *first:* Susan saw a movie about sharks.
   next: She has not swum in the ocean.

   _____

   _____

5. *first:* Phillip cleaned the wall and fixed the holes.
   next: He painted the wall.

   _____

   _____

6. *first:* Craig was playing basketball.
   next: He broke his arm.

   _____

   _____

■ **Quiz 2:** **Present perfect vs. present perfect progressive.**

These sentences are written in the present perfect. Where possible, cross out the verb and rewrite it, using the present perfect progressive.

has been reading
1. She ~~has read~~ her book since she finished dinner.

2. Mary has seen that movie four times.

3. Karen has taken several computer classes.

4. Paul has taken a class in American history since January.

5. Barbara has been sick since Monday.

6. Robert has worked on his report for two hours.

7. John has lived in New York for five years.

8. Michael has taught English at Carver High for nine years.

9. Tom has not visited his grandmother yet.

10. Ali has had his car since 1995.

11. Teresa has watched TV since she got home from school.

■ **Quiz 3:** **Simple past vs. past perfect.**

Use the simple past or the past perfect to complete the paragraph. In some blanks, either tense is possible.

Michael *(begin)* _____*began*_____ his college education in 1988 at the

University of California in Berkeley. He *(graduate)* _____ with a

degree in English in 1992. Before he *(choose)* _____ English as his

major, he *(try)* _____ engineering and philosophy. He

(decide) _____ to work for a few years before he

(go) _____ to graduate school. By the time he

(enroll) _____ at San Francisco State University in 1994, he

(gain) _____ valuable experience as a technical writer for a software

company. He *(take)* _____ four years to finish his Master's degree

in Communications because he *(give, not)* _____ up his job while he

was going to school. Many students *(finish)* _____ the program in

just two years, but Michael was sure his work experience would help him find a job.

■ **Quiz 4:**   Past perfect progressive and review of perfect tenses.

Decide if the sentence in quotation marks is correct or incorrect. If it is correct, write
Correct. If the sentence is incorrect, rewrite it.

1. You ate breakfast. Then you went to your friend's house. Your friend offers you
    breakfast. He asks, "Have you ever eaten breakfast?"

    _____*incorrect. Have you eaten breakfast yet?*_____

2. You are telling your friend about your vacation in Hawaii last summer. She asks
    you, "Did you see the large volcano?"

    _____

3. You and your friend are talking about where you want to go for dinner. You both
    like to try new types of food. Your friend asks you, "Have you ever had Indonesian
    food?"

    _____

4. You and your friend are talking about your jobs. You started your job in 1990, and
    you still work for the same company. You tell your friend, "I have started working
    since 1990."

    _____

5. You and your friend are discussing how your lives now are different from your lives
    in your home countries. You say to your friend, "I have been working as a doctor
    until I moved to this country."

    _____

6. You and your friend are watching the news about a terrible earthquake in Taiwan.
    You say to your friend, "I never was in a serious earthquake."

    _____

■ CHAPTER 3 TEST

A. Combine each pair of sentences, using *after, before, since,* or *while.*

1. *first:* Karen graduated from college.
   next: Karen has been working for First National Bank.
   _____*Since Karen graduated from college, she has been working for First National Bank.*_____

2. *first:* John had been working for ABC Oil Company.
   next: John took a job with First National Bank.
   _____

3. *first:* Karen was working for First National Bank.
   next: John joined the bank.
   _____

4. *first:* Karen began to work for the bank.
   next: Karen has dated several men.
   _____

5. *first:* Karen met John.
   next: Karen has not gone out with any other man.
   _____

6. *first:* John had already been married once.
   next: John met Karen.
   _____

7. *first:* John and Karen had been dating for a year.
   next: John asked Karen to marry him.
   _____

8. *first:* John and Karen got married.
   next: John and Karen looked for an apartment.
   _____

9. *first:* John and Karen were looking for an apartment.
   next: John lost his job at First National Bank.
   _____

10. *first:* John lost his job.
    next: John has gone back to school.
    _____

11. *first:* John got an advanced degree in economics.
    next: John has been teaching at the university.

    _____

B. Decide if the sentence in quotation marks is correct or incorrect. If it is correct, write **Correct**. If it is incorrect, rewrite the sentence.

1. Your friend John is telling you about an accident that almost happened to him. He says, "I was crossing the street while a car wasn't stopping at the stop light and almost was hitting me!"

    incorrect. While I was crossing the street, a car didn't stop at the stop light and

    almost hit me!   OR

    I was crossing the street when a car didn't stop at the stop light and almost

    hit me!

2. Your friend John is telling you about the very busy day he just had at work. He says, "While I was answering the telephone, people were asking me questions and giving me papers to take care of."

    _____

    _____

3. John is telling you about his experiences in the United States. He says, "Since I moved to the US, I have taken a mud bath, gone skydiving, and watched several baseball games."

    _____

    _____

4. John is telling you about the wonderful dinner he cooked last night for his parents. He says, "After we finished the salad, I served a tender and juicy roast beef."

    _____

    _____

5. John is telling you about his vacation last summer. He says, "After we visited the big island of Hawaii, we had been visiting Honolulu."

    _____

    _____

6. John is telling you more about last summer's vacation. He says, "We had been lying on the beaches for several days before we decided to go snorkeling."

_____

_____

7. John is telling you about his difficulty after giving up smoking. He says, "Since I had stopped smoking, I have gained over thirty pounds from eating candy."

_____

_____

8. John's car broke down while he was driving across the country. He doesn't understand why. He says, "I had carefully checked the oil and gas before I left on vacation."

_____

_____

9. John was studying in the library when something bad happened. He says, "While I was getting a drink of water, someone stole my math book."

_____

_____

10. John is explaining what he did when he discovered his math book was missing. "After I realized that my math book was gone, I was calling the campus police."

_____

_____

11. John is very upset about losing his math book. He tells you, "I have never been leaving my books on a library table since I lost my math book."

_____

_____

CHAPTER **4**
Future Time

■ **Quiz 1:** *Will* vs. *be going to.*

Use ***will*** and/or ***be going to*** with the verb in parentheses. Sometimes only one form is correct. Sometimes both forms can be used. Use contractions.

1. **A:** With your car in the shop, how are you going to get to work?

   B: I *(take)* _____*am going to take*_____ the bus. OR

   I *(ask)* _____ Alice to give me a ride.

2. **A:** It's starting to get a little chilly.

   B: I *(get)* _____ your sweater for you.

3. **A:** *(be)* _____ Ed _____ on time
   for the dinner?

   B: Don't worry. He *(arrive)* _____ early.

4. **A:** Have you made plans for New Year's Eve?

   B: Yes. We *(stay)* _____ in a hotel downtown and

   (attend) _____ a party at the art museum.

5. **A:** I need to stop at the library before we go to lunch.

   B: Fine. I *(meet)* _____ you on the front steps at noon.

   A: Great.

6. **A:** What are Fred's plans after graduation?

   B: He *(work)* _____ for a year before he goes to graduate
   school.

7. **A:** What are Gary's plans after graduation?

   B: He isn't sure. Perhaps he *(work)* _____ for a year, then
   begin graduate school.

8. **A:** What are you going to do this weekend?

   B: I *(clean, probably)* _____ the house and garage.

■ **Quiz 2:** Expressing the future in time clauses.

Combine the ideas in the pairs of sentences, using the adverb in parentheses.

1. *first:* Bob will get here soon.
   then: We will see Bob. *(when)*

   _____ *When Bob gets here, we will see him.* OR *We will see Bob when he gets here.* _____

2. *first:* We will paint the living room.
   then: We will buy new curtains. *(as soon as)*

   _____

   _____

3. *same time:* I am going to be at the supermarket.
   same time: I am going to buy a new dish pan. *(while)*

   _____

   _____

4. *first:* Linda is going to watch TV.
   then: Linda's parents will tell her to go to bed. *(until)*

   _____

   _____

5. *first:* Mr. Swan is going to teach an algebra class.
   then: Mr. Swan is going to teach a geometry class. *(before)*

   _____

   _____

6. *first:* I am going to sweep the kitchen floor.
   then: I am going to mop the kitchen floor. *(as soon as)*

   _____

   _____

7. *first:* Bob is going to buy his first car.
   then: Bob is going to give his friends a ride in his car. *(when)*

   _____

   _____

8. *same time:* Tom is going to finish his law degree.
   same time: Tom's wife is going to work. *(while)*

   _____

   _____

9. *first:* Gary is going to wash the dinner dishes.
   then: Gary is going to read in bed. *(after)*

   _____

   _____

10. *first:* The sun is going to come out.
    then: I am going to go sailing on the lake. *(when)*

    _____

    _____

11. *first:* Peter is going to finish his homework.
    then: Peter is going to see a movie. *(after)*

    _____

    _____

■ **Quiz 3:** **Using the simple present and present progressive to express future time.**

A. Indicate the meaning expressed by the *italicized* verbs by writing ***in the future,*** ***now,*** or ***habitually*** in the blanks.

1. I *am going* to go to England during winter break.   <u>*in the future*</u>

2. The plane *leaves* at 5:30 P.M.   _____

3. I *arrive* in London at noon the next day.   _____

4. I *am going* to go to Salisbury after I go to London.   _____

5. I *am reading* a travel book about England right now.   _____

6. I *go* to England every winter.   _____

B. Write the above sentences using different verb tenses, if possible. If it is not possible, write ***no change***.

1. I *am going* to go to England during winter break.

    <u>*No change.*</u>

2. The plane *leaves* at 5:30 P.M.

    _____

3. I *arrive* in London at noon the next day.

    _____

4. I *am going* to go to Salisbury after I *go to* London.

    _____

5. I *am reading* a travel book about England right now.

    _____

6. I *go* to England every winter.

    _____

■ **Quiz 4:** Future progressive.

Answer the question for each person, using the words in parentheses and the future progressive.

Question: What will you be doing at this time next year?

1. Jackie: *(work, for the same company)*

   _____I will be working for the same company._____

2. Maureen: *(start a family, with my husband)*

   _____

3. Tony: *(travel, in Africa)*

   _____

4. John: *(take classes, at my local community college)*

   _____

5. Patricia: *(build houses, in Ireland)*

   _____

6. Fred: *(write, my doctoral thesis)*

   _____

7. Sue: *(plan, my wedding)*

   _____

8. Mary: *(have a good time, in my retirement)*

   _____

9. Tom: *(look for, a new job)*

   _____

10. Bill: *(recover from, eye surgery)*

    _____

11. Ron: *(study engineering, at Georgetown University)*

    _____

■ **Quiz 5:**   **Future perfect and future perfect progressive.**

What do you think the world will be like a hundred years from now? What changes will or will not have occurred between then and now? Write your predictions for the following things, using the future perfect and the future perfect progressive.

1. Scientists, discover a cure for cancer

   _____ *Scientists will have discovered a cure for cancer.* _____

2. The European countries, become one nation

   _____

3. A major earthquake, destroy California

   _____

4. All sea life, die from pollution

   _____

5. A single world government, be established

   _____

6. The world population, exceed 100 billion

   _____

7. People, fly to Mars for vacations for many years

   _____

8. A meteor, kill all life on earth

   _____

9. Everyone, speak a single language since 2050

   _____

10. People, learn to live in peace and love

    _____

11. People, live on the moon for 50 years

    _____

■ CHAPTER 4 TEST

A. Combine each pair of sentences, using the adverb in parentheses.

1. *first:* Mary will work on her math homework.
   then: Mary will review her grammar lesson. *(after)*

   _____*Mary will review her grammar lesson after she works on her math homework.*_____

2. *first:* John will have graduated from college.
   then: John will turn 22 years old in June. *(before)*

   _____

3. *first:* Janice will have been working at the bank for thirty-seven years.
   then: Janice will retire in November. *(by the time)*

   _____

4. *first:* Margaret is going to travel in Asia.
   then: Margaret is going to visit her sister in Sydney, Australia. *(when)*

   _____

5. *same time:* Tony will be studying at the library tomorrow night.
   same time: Peter will be writing his book report at home. *(while)*

   _____

6. *first:* The ships will stay in the harbor.
   then: The tide will come in. *(until)*

   _____

7. *first:* Michael's airplane leaves tomorrow morning.
   then: Karen is going to catch a train for Washington. *(after)*

   _____

8. *first:* Betty is going to pick the ripe apples from her tree.
   then: Betty is going to use the apples for an apple pie. *(as soon as)*

   _____

9. *first:* Robert is going to grow up and find a job.
   then: Robert is going to find his own apartment. *(when)*

   _____

10. *first:* Mrs. Lee will have gone to bed.
    then: Her daughter will come home from her date. *(by the time)*

    _____

11. *same time:* Amy will be cleaning out the garage.
    same time: Her husband will be painting the front door. *(while)*

    _____

B. By this day next month, what things will have occurred in your life? Write predictions for the following topics, using the future perfect and the future perfect progressive. Write two sentences for each topic.

1. shopping

   _____ *I will have bought ten pounds of cat food.* OR _____

   _____ *I will have been shopping at Safeway for two months.* _____

2. cleaning

   _____

   _____

3. studying

   _____

   _____

4. exercising

   _____

   _____

5. eating

   _____

   _____

6. traveling

   _____

   _____

CHAPTER 5
Adverb Clauses of Time
and Review of Verb Tenses

■ **Quiz 1:** Adverb clauses and time relationships.

Complete the sentences with appropriate time adverbs. Add punctuation as necessary. If no adverb is needed, write Ø.

1. ____*Whenever*____ Martha drinks coffee late at night ____,_____

she cannot fall asleep ____*when*____ she goes to bed.

2. ____*Ø*____ Boris is going to clean the bathrooms

____*after*____ he mops the kitchen floor.

3. _____ Nancy doesn't practice for her interviews

_____ she won't get a job.

4. _____ Diane read a lot of car magazines _____
she chose the car that she wanted to buy.

5. _____ Tim stopped using a dictionary _____
he has made many spelling mistakes.

6. _____ Ms. Rodriguez finishes the business report

_____ she will fax a copy to the New York office.

7. _____ Steven was taking a nap _____ the
earthquake occurred.

8. _____ Prakash took the bus to work _____
he got to work an hour early.

9. _____ Jane is finished reading the newspaper

_____ she puts the newspaper in a bag for recycling.

10. _____ Nina washes the dog _____ she takes
a shower herself.

11. _____ Larry will reread his composition for errors

_____ he turns in his paper.

■ **Quiz 2:** **Verb tense review.**

Choose the best words to complete each sentence.

1. John ___c.___ for IBM since 1972.
   - a. is working
   - b. works
   - c. has worked

2. Elizabeth broke her leg while she _____ down a mountain.
   - a. was skiing
   - b. skied
   - c. had been skiing

3. The children _____ into the house when it began to rain.
   - a. had run
   - b. ran
   - c. are running

4. Every time Nancy _____ some money, she asks her father.
   - a. needs
   - b. needed
   - c. has needed

5. Kevin _____ very happy at his job until he got a new supervisor.
   - a. has been
   - b. had been
   - c. is

6. Jill _____ her family to Disneyland on vacation twelve times.
   - a. has taken
   - b. has been taking
   - c. takes

7. Olga will give her report to her boss as soon as she _____ a few figures.
   - a. checked
   - b. will check
   - c. checks

8. By the time Matthew finishes medical school, he _____ over $60,000 in student loans.
   - a. will have borrowed
   - b. will borrow
   - c. borrows

9. It _____ every day since our vacation started.
   - a. rained
   - b. has rained
   - c. rains

10. Before the guests arrived, Philip _____ most of the peanuts.
    - a. is already eating
    - b. has already eaten
    - c. had already eaten

11. The last time I _____ to Paris, I took a boat cruise on the Seine.
    - a. went
    - b. was going
    - c. have gone

■ CHAPTER 5 TEST

A. Combine each pair of sentences, using the adverb in parentheses. Pay attention to verb tense, meaning, and punctuation.

1. *first:* Teresa read a lot of college catalogs.
   then: Teresa chose the college that she wants to attend. *(after)*

   After Teresa read a lot of college catalogs, she chose the college she wants to attend.

2. *first:* We will be working on the new project.
   then: Our boss will return from his vacation. *(when)*

   _____

3. *first:* Joe will get up at 6 A.M.
   then: Joe will do his exercises. *(as soon as)*

   _____

4. *first:* Kathy will be living in Texas.
   then: Kathy's husband will return from his job in South America. *(when)*

   _____

5. *first:* I am going to pick up my cousin at the airport.
   then: I am going to show him the Golden Gate Bridge. *(after)*

   _____

6. *first:* Martina is going to go out to dinner with her friends for her birthday.
   then: Martina and her friends are going to go dancing at a night club. *(before)*

   _____

7. *first:* Maurice was eating lunch in a restaurant.
   then: Maurice dropped his napkin on the floor. *(when)*

   _____

8. *first:* Ann will get over her bad cold.
   then: Ann will return to work. *(as soon as)*

   _____

9. *first:* Mary rinses the food off the dishes.

 then: Mary puts the dishes in the dishwasher. *(after)*

 _____

10. *first:* Ali will have graduated from high school.

 then: Ali's brother will get married. *(by the time)*

 _____

11. *first:* The college started offering ESL courses.

 then: Becky has been studying ESL. *(since)*

 _____

B. Read the sentences. Then check the correct answers.

1. When Mary lost her purse, she was shopping at New Park Mall.
 What is the meaning?

 ❑ First, Mary loses her purse. Then, Mary shops.

 ❑ Mary loses her purse and shops at the same time.

 ☒ While shopping, Mary lost her purse.

 When does this action happen?

 ☒ Past

 ❑ Present habit

 ❑ Future

2. Before Mary sees the dentist, she flosses and brushes her teeth carefully.
 What is the meaning?

 ❑ First, Mary flosses and brushes. Then, Mary sees dentist.

 ❑ Mary flosses, brushes, and sees dentist at the same time.

 ❑ First, Mary sees dentist. Then, Mary flosses and brushes.

 When does this action happen?

 ❑ Past

 ❑ Present habit

 ❑ Future

3. If Mary wins the lottery, she is going to buy a new car for each of her sisters and brothers.
 What is the meaning?

 ❑ Maybe Mary wins lottery. Then Mary buys cars.

 ❑ Mary wins lottery and buys cars at the same time.

 ❑ Maybe Mary buys cars. Then Mary wins lottery.

 When does this action happen?

 ❑ Past

 ❑ Present habit

 ❑ Future

4. Mary will separate the bottles and cans for recycling before she puts out the garbage.

What is the meaning?

- ❑ First, Mary puts out garbage. Then, Mary separates things.
- ❑ Mary puts out garbage and separates things at the same time.
- ❑ First, Mary separates things. Then, Mary puts out garbage.

When does this action happen?

- ❑ Past
- ❑ Present habit
- ❑ Future

5. While Mary was riding the bus home from work, she was listening to music on her Walkman.

What is the meaning?

- ❑ First, Mary rides bus. Then, Mary listens to music.
- ❑ Mary rides and listens at the same time.
- ❑ First, Mary listens to music. Then, Mary rides bus.

When does this action happen?

- ❑ Past
- ❑ Present habit
- ❑ Future

6. John does his homework after he watches TV.

What is the meaning?

- ❑ First, John does homework. Then, John watches TV.
- ❑ John does homework and watches TV at the same time.
- ❑ First, John watches TV. Then, John does homework.

When does this action happen?

- ❑ Past
- ❑ Present habit
- ❑ Future

CHAPTER 6
Subject-Verb Agreement

■ **Quiz 1:** **Basic subject–verb agreement.**

Choose the correct answer in parentheses.

1. The chickens on the farm *(lays, (lay))* 200 eggs a day.

2. Every student *(needs, need)* to show proof of residency.

3. Each seam and button *(is, are)* carefully checked before the clothing is shipped to stores.

4. The computer available in stores now *(doesn't, don't)* run as fast as the computer available on the Internet.

5. Three representatives from each country *(is, are)* attending the economic meeting.

6. Practicing the piano several hours a day *(is, are)* necessary if you want to become a professional player.

7. Plants and animals *(requires, require)* water to survive.

8. The lights that Michael installed along the path *(makes, make)* the steps much safer.

9. Watching TV *(has, have)* fallen in popularity since ten years ago.

10. Martha and her two sisters *(leaves, leave)* for vacation next Monday.

11. Alex, as well as his two brothers, *(is, are)* coming home on Saturday.

■ Quiz 2:   Subject–verb agreement: using expressions of quantity.

Decide if the sentence is correct or incorrect. If it is correct, write *Correct*. If it is incorrect, rewrite the sentence.

1. Has any of the students taken this class before?

   _____*incorrect. Have any of the students taken this class before?*_____

2. A number of volunteers are needed to finish this cleaning project.

   _____

3. Some of the stolen jewelry was recovered two weeks later.

   _____

4. A lot of my friends recommends this apartment complex.

   _____

5. None of my friends thinks I should sell my car.

   _____

6. The number of restaurants in San Francisco exceed 2,000.

   _____

7. Each of these bowls are worth more than $150.

   _____

8. All of the money really belongs to that man over there.

   _____

9. One of my pencil needs to be sharpened.

   _____

10. Half of the airplanes leaves on time.

    _____

11. Every one of the children need love and affection.

    _____

■ Quiz 3:   Subject–verb agreement: using *there + be.*

Using **there** and **be,** write two sentences to name things that are found in each of these places.

1. in a wallet

_____*There are credit cards in a wallet. There is money in a wallet.*_____

_____

2. in a library

_____

_____

3. on a beach

_____

_____

4. in a post office

_____

_____

5. in a kitchen

_____

_____

6. on an airplane

_____

_____

■ **Quiz 4:** Subject–verb agreement: some irregularities.

Choose the correct answer in parentheses.

1. Two hundred miles (*take,* (*takes*)) three hours by car.

2. The people in my company (*come, comes*) from many different countries.

3. The Chinese (*is, are*) the inventors of gun powder and noodles.

4. The Netherlands (*is, are*) located north of Germany.

5. The homeless (*has, have*) little chance of finding a job.

6. Japanese (*is, are*) a difficult language to learn because of the different alphabets.

7. The statistics about the economy (*is, are*) not good this month.

8. Politics (*is, are*) the major topic of conversation in the nation's capital.

9. Today's newspaper (*has, have*) an interesting article about the causes of diabetes.

10. The police (*is, are*) called whenever there is a murder.

11. The news from my cousins (*is, are*) not good.

■ CHAPTER 6 TEST

A. Circle the best choice to complete each sentence. The first one is done for you.

My favorite place *(be, (is,) are)* a beautiful island called Tranquila. *(It, Its, There)* is located 50 miles east of the coast of Florida. The weather on the island *(be, is, are)* very warm all year. There *(is, are, has, have)* a little rain every afternoon, but each rain storm *(lasts, last, lasting)* only about 30 minutes. Beautiful white sand beaches *(surrounds, surround, surrounding)* the island. The mountains at the center of the island *(be, is, are)* also wonderful.

The people on Tranquila *(be, is, are)* very friendly to visitors. *(It's, There are, Its, They are)* happy to give directions to the beach or to the shopping district. Many stores *(sells, sell, selling)* beautiful jewelry. The jewelry *(be, is, are)* beautiful and cheap, and twenty dollars *(buys, buy, buying)* a necklace that can cost over a hundred dollars at home. *(There has, There have, There is, There are)* so many wonderful stores. Make sure you save a lot of time for shopping. Even four hours *(be, is, are)* not enough! If you collect seashells, don't look in the stores. The beaches on Tranquila *(be, is, are)* covered with seashells. You can pick them up for free, so the stores *(are not, does not, do not)* sell them.

Tranquila is a quiet island. Because *(it is, it has, there is, there has)* small and far away from other places, *(there hasn't, there haven't, there isn't, there aren't)* any televisions or radios. News *(be, is, are)* available only from day-old newspapers from the mainland. *(There has, There have, There is, There are)* little crime in Tranquila. The police *(are not, does not, do not)* have much to do except give directions to tourists. Drinking *(be, is, are)* illegal on Tranquila. The number of arrests *(be, is, are)* fewer than three a year. Tranquila has very little pollution, too. *(Its, They are, It's, There are)* a few cars and trucks, but most people like to walk.

Every visitor *(comes, come, coming)* back from Tranquila happy and well-rested. All people really *(enjoys, enjoy, enjoying)* the charms of Tranquila and want to visit again soon.

B. Decide if the sentence is correct or incorrect. If it is correct, write *Correct.* If it is incorrect, rewrite the sentence.

1. How many student are there in this classroom?

   _____*incorrect. How many students are there in this classroom?*_____

2. Every answer on your quiz needs to be checked carefully.

   _____

3. I don't know how to correct one of the mistake on my quiz.

   _____

4. There are a lot of expensive clothing in that store.

   _____

5. Thirty minutes is not enough to finish this quiz.

   _____

6. French is the most popular foreign language at my school.

   _____

7. Is the Chinese the most difficult language that you have ever studied?

   _____

8. Studying all night before quizzes are not a good way to learn.

   _____

9. The flowers in my garden needs a lot of water every day.

   _____

10. The children in my neighborhood do not have a good place to play.

    _____

11. Growing roses are my neighbor's specialty.

    _____

CHAPTER 7
Nouns

■ **Quiz 1:** Regular and irregular plural nouns.

Complete each sentence with the plural form of the noun in parentheses.

1. On Friday night, John rented two _____*videos*_____ to watch during the weekend. *(video)*

2. Michael is only 10 years old, but he is already five _____ tall. *(foot)*

3. Catherine played the same piece on several different _____ before she chose which piano to buy. *(piano)*

4. We need to put out steak _____ because we are having roast beef for dinner. *(knife)*

5. When our house caught on fire, the firemen sprayed water on our neighbors'
_____ to stop the fire from spreading. *(roof)*

6. My uncle's ranch has more than 200 cattle and 150 _____. *(sheep)*

7. Mr. Lee's alarm system has protected his jewelry store from
_____. *(thief)*

8. You can see many _____ around the tracks in the subway station. *(mouse)*

9. The desert scenery is beautiful because of its simplicity, with only sand and
_____ as far as the eye can see. *(cactus)*

10. The prime minister had to deal with several political _____ as soon as he took office. *(crisis)*

11. The dentist is going to clean Mary's _____ when she visits him next Tuesday. *(tooth)*

■ **Quiz 2:** Possessive nouns and noun modifiers.

    A. Complete each sentence with the possessive form of the noun in parentheses.

    1. The teacher collected the _____*students'*_____ papers at the end of the test.
       (students)

    2. I am going with Linda to a party at a _____ house this Saturday.
       (friend)

    3. _____ dog has been missing for two weeks. *(Doris)*

    4. Did you read about the terrible earthquake in _____ newspaper?
       (this morning)

    5. You can find _____ sportswear on the third floor of the store.
       (men)

    6. The nurse was reviewing the _____ charts when the doctor
       asked for her assistance. *(patients)*

    B. Answer the questions, using a noun modifier. Use the words in **boldface** to form your answer.

    1. Steven spends every Saturday working in his **garden**. He grows many different kinds of **vegetables**. Where does Steven work every Saturday?

       _____*In his vegetable garden*_____

    2. When John gets home from work in the **afternoon**, he usually takes a **nap**. It makes him feel refreshed. What does John enjoy doing after work?

       _____*Taking a*_____

    3. Ron rides his **bicycle** to the train station each morning. There are special **racks** in front of the station where he can lock it up. Where does Ron leave his bicycle when he takes the train?

       _____*In a*_____

    4. During the week, Sally works in an office. On weekends, she is a **coach** for her daughter's **volleyball** team. What is Sally's job on weekends?

       _____*She is a*_____

    5. Mr. and Mrs. Tran have four children, and Mrs. Tran's mother lives with them. They would like to find a **house** that has **four bedrooms**. What are Mr. and Mrs. Tran looking for?

       _____*A*_____

    6. Pamela is going to pay for her groceries by **check**. The groceries cost **fifteen dollars**. How is Pamela going to pay?

       _____*With a*_____

■ **Quiz 3:** **Count and noncount nouns.**

Add final *-s/-es* to the nouns in *italics* if necessary. Do not add or change any other words.

Foreston is a former industrial town that is trying to create new *job*ˢ∧ and build a healthy *economy*. Foreston is located on a wide river and used to be surrounded by *forest*, which made it an ideal place for the production of *paper* and wood *product*. By 1980, the *hill* around Foreston were empty of *tree*, the factories had closed, and the river was unsafe because of *pollution*. To create new jobs, local *citizen* and city leaders are trying to attract health and technology *company* by offering low *tax* and cheap *housing*. Local citizens are also concerned about the environment. School groups have cleaned *garbage* out of the river, and the water is safe again for *swimming* and fishing. Every week, volunteers climb the nearby slopes and plant new saplings and scatter wildflower *seed*. With *patience*, they hope that they will see Foreston surrounded by tall pines, birches, and oaks once again.

■ **Quiz 4:** **Article usage.**

Circle the best choice to complete each sentence. Add capital letters if necessary.

1. Last Saturday, I needed to clean my *(a, an, the, some, Ⓞ)* messy office. My desk was covered with *(a mail, mail, some mails, the mails)*, scraps of paper, coins, and *(a, an, the, some, Ø)* old magazines. I had old *(newspaper, some newspapers, newspapers)* on the floor and old files on a chair. I took *(a, an, the, some, Ø)* mail and threw it away. I sorted *(a, an, the, some, Ø)* scraps of paper and put them in *(a, an, the, some, Ø)* neat stack by the telephone. I put *(a change, change, some change, the change)* into my pocket. I looked through *(a, an, the, some, Ø)* old magazines and newspapers, and I decided to put most of them in *(a, an, the, some, Ø)* recycling box. Finally, I put *(a, an, the, some, Ø)* files back in the filing cabinet in their correct places.

2. People collect *(a, an, the, some, Ø)* things for different reasons. Most people hope their collection will increase in value. Many people collect *(a, an, the, some, Ø)* stamps and *(a, an, the, some, Ø)* artwork. My aunt has *(a, an, the, some, Ø)* unusual painting that she bought for ten dollars. It is now worth over two hundred dollars. *(A, An, The, Some, Ø)* people want to remember vacations and trips. *(A, An, The, Some, Ø)* postcards and *(a, an, the, some, Ø)* foreign money are very popular souvenirs. I have *(a, an, the, some, Ø)* friend who collects *(a, an, the, some, Ø)* rocks. He has *(a, an, the, some, Ø)* different story to tell about each rock.

■ **Quiz 5:** Expressions of quantity and *few, a few, little, a little.*

    A. Add ***much*** or ***many*** to complete each sentence.

      1. I don't have _____*much*_____ time to finish my homework.

      2. When I asked him for advice, he didn't have _____ suggestions.

      3. When I was in college, I didn't know _____ people.

      4. You don't need to add _____ salt to this soup.

      5. You don't have to spend _____ money to get a good camera.

      6. This article doesn't have _____ facts.

    B. For each sentence above, write a sentence that has a similar meaning. Use the word in parentheses and ***a few, few, a little,*** or ***little.***

      1. (*minute*) _____*I have only a few minutes to finish my homework.*_____

      _____

      2. (*advice*) _____

      _____

      3. (*friend*) _____

      _____

      4. (*spice*) _____

      _____

      5. (*dollar*) _____

      _____

      6. (*information*) _____

      _____

■ **Quiz 6:** Using *of* in expressions of quantity, including *all* and *both*.

Some (but not all) of these sentences contain errors in the use of expressions of quantity. Find and correct the errors.

                                  the

1. The bank puts all of ∧ money into a safe when it closes at night.

2. Both the telephones didn't work well, so Mary returned them to the store.

3. All children need a good night's sleep and a good breakfast to do well in school.

4. Both of children and adults should visit a dentist twice a year.

5. A few of the exercises are not good for people with heart trouble.

6. Susan left both of the books for her math class in the classroom.

7. This store accepts both of credit cards and traveler's checks.

8. Kevin looked in all the rooms of his apartment, but he still couldn't find his keys.

9. People smoking in bed caused both of fires last night.

10. Most of parking spaces in the parking lot are full.

11. John finished some of the homework from his English class.

■ **Quiz 7:** *One, each,* and *every.*

Rewrite each sentence, using the expression of quantity plus the singular or plural form of the noun.

1. *(every / the city)* Wendy enjoyed . . . she visited during her vacation.

   Wendy enjoyed every one of the cities she visited during her vacation.

2. *(every / night)* John watches a different movie . . .

   John watches a different movie every night.

3. *(each / the direction)* Peter followed . . . very carefully when he baked his first cake.

   _____

4. *(each / weekend)* Cathy plays soccer . . .

   _____

5. *(one / word)* Robert spelled only . . . incorrectly on the test.

   _____

6. *(each / student)* . . . needs to bring a dictionary to the next class.

   _____

7. *(every / the member)* . . . voted for Nina as the president of the club.

   _____

8. *(one / the problem)* . . . facing big cities is homelessness.

   _____

9. *(every / light)* Thomas turns off . . . in the house before he goes to bed.

   _____

10. *(one / pill)* The doctor told Steven to take . . . every six hours.

    _____

11. *(one / the book)* Betty found . . . at the library.

    _____

■ CHAPTER 7 TEST

A. For each sentence, write a sentence that has a similar meaning. Use the word in *italics* to replace the word in **boldface**.

1. Martha receives many **letters** because she regularly writes all of her friends. *(mail)*

    Martha receives much mail because she writes regularly to all her friends.

2. Brian was late to work because there were so many **cars** on the road. *(traffic)*

    _____

3. In our math class, we receive a lot of **assignments** to do before the next class. *(homework)*

    _____

4. **All** of the children need to get shots before they start school. *(every)*

    _____

5. John had to wait only **a few** minutes before his doctor was free to see him. *(a little)*

    _____

6. My three-year-old nephew doesn't eat **much** rice at dinner. *(a little)*

    _____

7. Pearl brought too many **suitcases** for her plane flight, so she had to pay an extra charge. *(luggage)*

    _____

8. Sam wrote **all** of the new vocabulary words on cards so that he could review them on the bus. *(each)*

    _____

9. The police still do not have many **details** about how the fire started. *(information)*

    _____

10. Sandra earns only **a little** money at her job in the restaurant. *(much)*

    _____

11. When Gloria went to the zoo yesterday, she didn't take **many** pictures. *(few)*

    _____

B. Circle the best choice to complete each sentence. The first one is done for you.

A Busy Day at Home

Last Monday was *(a, an, the, some, Ø)* holiday, so I didn't have to go to work. I had *(much thing, many thing, much things, many things)* to do, and I was happy to have *(few, a few, little, a little)* time to finish all my chores. First I needed to rearrange *(one, one of, some, some of)* the furniture in the living room, which was too crowded. I moved *(one of chair, one of the chairs, one of chairs)* from the living room into the *(guests bedroom, guest bedroom, bedroom guest)*. I moved another chair into my *(son, sons, son's, sons')* room. I put *(a, an, the, some, Ø)* chair in the corner for him to sit and read books in. I moved *(a, an, the, some, Ø)* only sofa in *(a, an, the, some, Ø)* living room against the wall. Now the living room was less crowded.

Next, I needed to clean *(some thing, some of thing, some things, some of things)* in the kitchen. First, I cleaned out *(a, an, the, some, Ø)* refrigerator. I had *(a lot, lots of, a lots of, lot of)* leftover food, and some of it was very old. I threw away *(a, an, some, some of)* rotten tomatoes, *(a, an, some, some of)* old bread, a piece of dried-up chicken, and an open can of soda. I also found *(few, little, a few, a little)* grapes in the back of the refrigerator. I didn't know how long they had been there. I wiped off *(a, an, the, Ø)* inside of the *(vegetable, vegetables, vegetables')* drawer and the *(meat, meats, meat's)* drawer. Then, I swept and mopped *(a, an, the, some, Ø)* floor. I also scrubbed *(a, an, the, some, Ø)* kitchen sink.

After lunch, I did *(a, an, the, some, Ø)* work in my backyard. I mowed the lawn and pulled *(a lot, a lots, a lot of, a lots of)* weeds. I trimmed the branches on *(each my bush, each of my bush, each my bushes, each of my bushes)*. I also needed to prune two *(rose bush, rose bushes, roses bush, roses bushes)*. The first one was easy to prune, but *(another, other, the other, others)* had many thorns. I stuck myself several times. Finally, I planted *(a, an, the, some, Ø)* flowers around *(a, an, the, some, Ø)* front door.

It was 3 P.M. I was exhausted, but very happy. I had finished *(all, all of, all my)* chores. My house and my garden looked wonderful. I couldn't wait to see my *(family, family's, families')* faces when they came home from their trip to the zoo.

CHAPTER **8**
Pronouns

■ **Quiz 1:** **Personal pronouns.**

Choose the correct words in parentheses.

1. (*(I,)* *me, my, mine*) gave Tom (*I,* *(me,)* *my, mine*) piece of pie because (*(he,)* *him, his*) asked (*I,* *(me,)* *my, mine*).

2. Yesterday, Susan left (*she, her, hers*) purse on the bus when (*she, her, hers*) went downtown.

3. Mary got a bad grade on (*she, her, hers*) test in Mr. Thomas's class. (*She, Her, Hers*) is going to talk to (*he, him, his*) during (*he, him, his*) office hours tomorrow.

4. Grace and Karl took (*they, them, their, theirs*) baby to the doctor for a check-up. (*They, Them, Their, Theirs*) need to take (*he, him, his*) in every four months.

5. John doesn't want anybody to touch (*he, him, his*) things, and Julie doesn't want anyone to touch (*she, her, hers*).

6. (*We, Us, Our, Ours*) are worried that no one will come to our party because no one has called us yet.

7. Barbara went to (*she, her, hers*) nephew's birthday party yesterday. (*She, Her, Hers*) gave (*he, him, his*) a book that a friend of (*she, her, hers*) had recommended.

8. Teresa bought a sweater as a gift. She is going to give it to (*his, her*) brother. She also bought some towels. She is going to give (*it, them*) to a friend as a wedding present.

9. If (*you, your, yours*) don't finish (*you, your, yours*) homework on time, the teacher will ask (*you, your, yours*) to correct it by yourself.

■ **Quiz 2:** Personal pronoun agreement: generic, indefinite, and collective.

A. Rewrite the sentences, using a singular generic noun instead of a plural noun when appropriate. Some nouns can remain plural in order to express a general meaning.

1. Women have fewer opportunities in business than men do. If women do not own their own companies, it is unlikely that they will ever become president or CEO of these companies.

   A woman has fewer opportunities in business than a man does. If a woman does

   not own her own company, it is unlikely that she will ever become president or

   CEO of this company.

2. According to the Hippocratic Oath, doctors are never supposed to harm their patients. As a result, doctors have a difficult moral dilemma when patients ask to be allowed to die.

   _____

   _____

   _____

3. Bus drivers have one of the most stressful jobs in major cities. In addition to fighting traffic, drivers need to deal with angry customers, passengers who try to sneak on without paying a fare, and teenagers who play their music too loud.

   _____

   _____

   _____

4. Zoos can be very educational places. They give people an opportunity to see animals from distant lands. In zoos, people might see hippopotamuses, grizzly bears, white tigers, and elephants.

   _____

   _____

   _____

5. People should see their dentists twice a year. Dentists clean their teeth, but they also check for diseases and infections that can cause tooth decay and potential problems in the mouth.

_____

_____

_____

6. Computers have become standard business tools throughout most of the world. They are used to do calculations and word processing, but they are also used for communication and design.

_____

_____

_____

B. Complete the sentences with pronouns. In some of the sentences, there is more than one possibility. Choose the appropriate singular or plural verb if necessary.

1. The public should be aware of the dangers that this new power plant can cause. The government needs to inform _____*them*_____ of the risks that this project carries.

2. The class is too big to fit in this room. The school either needs to move

_____ into a larger room or split _____ into two smaller classes.

3. Most of the faculty is going to come to the president's meeting. _____

(want, wants) to find out about the new Internet use policy.

4. On the game show, the young couple won a trip to Hawaii. _____ also received a new set of dishes and a color TV.

5. The committee consists of representatives from different parts of the city.

_____ even _____ *(include, includes)* members from the financial

district and the industrial area.

6. My family is quite tall. All of _____, including the women, *(are, is)* over

5′10″.

■ **Quiz 3:**   **Reflexive pronouns.**

Complete the sentences, using the words in parentheses (if any) and the appropriate reflexive pronouns. Pay attention to verb tense.

1. When John fell down the stairs, he *(hurt)* _____*hurt himself*_____ very badly.

2. While Alex was working on his car, he *(cut)* _____ on a sharp edge.

3. I didn't think that I would, but I really *(enjoy)* _____ at Karen's party last night.

4. The members of the team are very proud of _____ after winning the city championship.

5. George *(kill)* _____ after his business went bankrupt.

6. Mary *(promise)* _____ that she would do better next time.

7. Because the food was included in the price of the trip, we *(stop, not)* _____ _____ from eating everything that we could.

8. I always *(talk to)* _____ about important things that I am thinking about.

9. Because they had been working so hard, they *(allow)* _____ a ten-minute break.

10. Rita was very angry at _____ for missing the important meeting.

11. If you *(take care of, not)* _____, no one will.

■ Quiz 4:   Impersonal pronouns.

A. Write the meanings of the pronoun in *italics*. Indicate whether the pronoun refers to everyone, anyone, or a specific person(s).

1. If *you* go swimming immediately after *you* eat a big meal, *you* may get cramps.

   _____*everyone*_____

2. If *you* call me from the airport, I will pick *you* up. Then *you* won't need to take a

   taxi. _____

3. I like to go to the library on Wednesdays because *they* always put out the new books on that day. By Thursday, *they* don't have any new books left to check out.

   _____

4. When *you* dial out, if *you* are dialing long distance, first *you* need to dial 9 and then the area code and the number. If *you* are dialing a local number, first dial 8 and

   then the number. _____

5. *You* can't just go through life and hope that good things will happen to *you*. *You*

   have to make *your* own happiness. _____

6. I need *you* to help me hang this picture. Can *you* tell me when the picture is

   straight? _____

B. Change these sentences from specific to general by using **one**.

1. John, you need to work harder if you want to succeed.

   _____*One needs to work harder if one wants to succeed.*_____

   _____

   _____

2. Sometimes, son, your memories are all that you have, so take good care of your photographs and mementos.

   _____

   _____

   _____

3. You should never talk on a cellular phone while you are driving. You might be distracted and get into an accident.

   _____

   _____

   _____

4. If you want to remember your dreams, you should keep a notebook next to your bed and write down all your thoughts the moment you wake up.

   _____

   _____

   _____

5. If you run out of gas on a bridge, you will receive a $100 fine and be charged for the tow to a gas station.

   _____

   _____

   _____

6. Karen, if you don't have good health, you can't have a good life.

   _____

   _____

   _____

■ **Quiz 5:** Forms of *other*.

Complete the sentences with a form of **other**.

1. **Waitress:** For dessert, we have a wonderful apple pie.

   Customer: I really don't like pie. What _____*other*_____ desserts do you have?

2. Some people like milk in their coffee. _____ like cream.

3. **Customer:** Excuse me. I dropped my napkin on the floor. May I have

   _____?

   Waitress: I'll bring one right away.

4. **Waitress:** There are two specials on the menu tonight. The first is a delicious

   broiled sea bass. _____ is an oven-roasted chicken with rosemary.

   Customer: I'll have the bass, please.

5. **Waitress:** Are you ready to order?

   Customer: There will be five of us, but only three of us are here. We'll wait until

   _____ arrive before we order.

6. **Waitress 1:** What a horrible day!

   Waitress 2: What happened?

   Waitress 1: Well, at one table, a child kicked me when I was walking by, and I

   dropped a tray of drinks. Later, _____ child wouldn't

   stop screaming, and all the _____ customers were very annoyed. AND I had a table of eight people who left me a tip of only $2!

7. A typical restaurant has a wide selection of condiments. One condiment is

ketchup. Another is mustard. _____ condiments include steak
sauce, Tabasco sauce, and Worcestershire sauce.

8. **Customer:** Excuse me. We've been waiting longer than that party, but they're
being seated first.

Waitress: I'm sorry, sir. You have a party of five and need a large table.

_____ people are only three and can fit at a smaller

table.

9. **Mary:** Where should we go for dinner?

John: How about the Red Sail Seafood Restaurant on the waterfront?

Mary: Have you ever eaten there? Is it any good?

John: I've never eaten there, but many _____ have and recommend
it highly.

10. **Customer:** We've been waiting fifteen minutes for a table. How much longer will
it be?

Waitress: Thank you for your patience. It should be only _____
five minutes at the most.

11. **Waitress:** And what would the children like to drink?

Customer: She'll have a root beer, and _____ will have milk.

Name _____ Class _____ Date _____

■ Quiz 6:   Expressions with *other*.

Correct the errors in the use of ***other***. (Some of the sentences are correct.)

1. I swim on Sundays, Tuesdays, and Thursdays. I go to the swimming pool every
   other
   ~~another~~ day.

2. My mother told me that in a good relationship, the two people communicate with
   each other, help one other, and forgive each other.

3. Did I tell you about running into Louis another day? I was at the bank, and he
   walked in to make a deposit. We had a nice chat.

4. Other than fish, no another pets are allowed in this apartment building.

5. During the war, my mother and father wrote to each another every day. In fact,
   they still have all their letters.

6. Jenny cheered as the members of her team ran across the finish line, one after the
   other.

7. Before I can help you with the budget report, I have to finish this project summary,
   check the data for the web page, review the profit projections for this month, and
   meet with the vice-president about the new product release. In another words, I
   can't help you until tomorrow at the earliest.

8. John can't go with us to the museum on Thursday, so he will have to see the
   exhibition of Impressionist paintings on the other day.

9. I'm almost done with using the computer. It will only take other ten minutes.
   Then you can use it.

10. My job working on an assembly line is very boring. All day long, I put together an
    electric circuit. They come down the line, one after another, and I put them
    together.

11. I don't need another haircut yet. I just got one the another morning.

■ CHAPTER 8 TEST

A. Complete the sentences with pronouns. The pronouns must refer to the word in *italics*.

1. *Robert* is taking classes at Clearwater College this semester. Last year,

    _____*he*_____ was working at a car factory in Milpitas. (1) _____ didn't

    enjoy (2) _____ job.

2. Many *people* find a great job after (3) _____ go back to school and finish

    (4) _____ degree.

3. *We* used to live in Kansas, where the land is very flat and rich. (5) _____

    had a wonderful vegetable garden behind (6) _____ house.

4. *Someone* left (7) _____ dictionary in the classroom last Friday.

    (8) _____ can go to the department office to claim (9) _____
    book.

5. *Personal computers* have changed education. When (10) _____ were

    invented in the early 1980s, (11) _____ cost more than $2,000 each.

    Today, people can buy (12) _____ in department stores, discount stores,
    and on the Internet.

6. If *one* drives above the speed limit, (13) _____ should expect to get a

    speeding ticket. When the police officer gives (14) _____ a ticket,

    (15) _____ should just accept it quietly.

7. Have you seen my *purse?* I left (16) _____ on this desk.

    (17) _____ is brown with a gold clasp. My sister bought

    (18) _____ for me for my last birthday.

8. I want *everyone* at my party to have a good time. (19) _____ should get

plenty to eat and drink. If (20) _____ want to take off

(21) _____ shoes, that's okay with me. The important thing is that

(22) _____ should enjoy (23) _____.

9. The *government* announced last night that (24) _____ was going to help

the earthquake victims in the south. (25) _____ voted to approve $100

million in assistance and supplies. Many people were surprised at

(26) _____ quick action because (27) _____ had responded so

slowly when the last earthquake occurred.

10. A *professor* has many responsibilities. First and foremost, (28) _____ has

an obligation to help students learn. Second, (29) _____ should do

research in (30) _____ field that will bring in research money and

improve the prestige of the college.

B. Using a form of **other** and some of your own words, make a sentence.

1. *eat, pie*

   Would you like to have another piece of pie?   OR _____

   Can you eat another piece of pie?   OR

   I can't eat another piece of pie.

2. *love, each*

   _____

3. *day, go*

   _____

4. *have, any, friends*

   _____

5. *need, five minutes*

   _____

6. *visit, every*

   _____

7. *buy, washing machine*

   _____

8. *than, pass*

   _____

9. *eat, prefer*

   _____

10. *chance, take*

    _____

11. *talk, one*

    _____

CHAPTER 9
Modals, Part 1

■ **Quiz 1:**   **Polite requests:** *I, you,* and *would you mind.*

Write an appropriate polite request for each of these situations.

1. You forgot your grammar book, and you want to borrow the teacher's. What do you say to the teacher?

    _____ *Could I borrow your grammar book?* _____ OR _____

    _____ *May I borrow your grammar book?* _____ OR _____

    _____ *Would you mind if I borrowed your grammar book?* _____

2. You are sitting in your friend's car. Your friend is driving. Your friend has turned the air conditioning on high, and you are feeling very cold. What do you say to your friend?

    _____

    _____

    _____

3. You are in a restaurant in the non-smoking section. A man at the next table lights a cigarette. What do you say to him?

    _____

    _____

    _____

4. You didn't do well on the last chapter quiz, and you have many questions for the teacher. You want to talk to her during her office hour, but you are worried that she will be busy. What do you say to her?

    _____

    _____

    _____

5. You get on the train. There is only one empty seat, but a young man has put his backpack on the seat. You want to sit down. What do you say to him?

_____

_____

_____

6. You call your friend Susan, but her mother tells you that she isn't home. You have some very important news for Susan, and you want to leave a message. What do you say to Susan's mother?

_____

_____

_____

■ **Quiz 2:** Necessity, lack of necessity, and prohibition.

Use *must*, *have to*, *must not*, or *don't have to* to complete the sentences.

1. **A:** Did you go to the movies last night?

   B: No, I _____*had to*_____ study for a test in math today.

2. **A:** When _____ we _____ turn in our quarterly reports?
   B: I think they're due on the 15th.

3. Here is the last point in my safety lecture. You _____ operate these machines if your hands are wet. You could get a serious shock.

4. **A:** I'm surprised to see you on the bus. Is your car still having problems?

   B: Yeah. I _____ take it to the garage, but I never seem to find time.

5. **A:** I'm so relieved!
   B: Why?
   A: Originally, our essays were due on Friday, but the teacher has put off the due

   date. Now we _____ hand them in until next Wednesday.

6. **A:** You aren't leaving the party already, are you?

   B: I'm really sorry, but I _____ go. I've had a wonderful time.
   A: See you soon.

7. **A:** I think everything is ready.

   B: This presentation is very important if we want to attract new business. There

   _____ be any problems.

   A: Don't worry, sir. I'm sure everything is ready.

8. **A:** I'm going to leave work early today. I _____ see my doctor.

   B: Are you sick?

   A: Last night, I _____ wake up every hour to blow my nose or take some more cough medicine. I barely slept.

   B: It sounds like you have the flu. Take care of yourself.

9. **A:** I think we can finish this by ourselves now. You _____ stay. You can go home.

   B: I can stay longer. I _____ do anything else tonight.

   A: Thanks, but you've worked long enough. Go home and put your feet up.

■ **Quiz 3:** Advisability: *should, ought to, had better,* and *should have.*

Read each story. Write what you think the person in each situation ***should have*** done or ***should not have*** done and what he or she ***should*** do or ***should not*** do now. Write two sentences for each story.

1. Michael and a friend stayed up late watching a movie. The next morning, Michael fell asleep on the train to work. When he woke up, he had already passed his stop. By the time he caught a train to go back, he would be late for work.

   _____*Michael should not have fallen asleep.*_____ OR _____

   _____*Michael should not have stayed up so late.*_____

   _____*Michael should call his boss and apologize.*_____ OR _____

   _____*Michael should call a taxi and try to get to work on time.*_____

2. Karen started using the Internet, and she discovered all the different stores there. Many of them offered really good bargains. Karen bought books, CDs, toys for her nephews, computer equipment, and even a TV. Karen just got her credit card bill. She found she had spent more than $2,500 last month. She is shocked.

   _____

   _____

   _____

3. At Silvia and Robert's wedding in July, there were more than 200 guests. Silvia put off writing thank-you notes for the wedding gifts she and Robert received. Now it is December. Silvia STILL hasn't sent out her thank-you notes.

_____

_____

_____

4. Jane got a puppy for her ten-year-old son, Kevin, who really wanted a dog and promised to take care of it himself. Kevin really loves his dog, but it has become Jane's job to take care of it and walk it. Kevin is always too busy or forgets.

_____

_____

_____

5. Mr. and Mrs. Taylor read about a new play at the City Theater. Mr. Taylor promised to buy tickets. Unfortunately, he always had to do something else first. When he finally went to the box office two weeks later, the show was sold out. His wife was very disappointed.

_____

_____

_____

6. Marcia went shopping for a new suitcase with her mother. Marcia's mother recommended that she buy the TravelPro suitcase for $250. Marcia's mother had one, and she said it was very good quality. A similar suitcase was on sale for $100, so Marcia bought the cheaper suitcase. Within a year, the suitcase lost a wheel and a zipper broke. Marcia's mother's TravelPro suitcase is still in good condition and works well.

_____

_____

_____

Name _____ Class _____ Date _____

■ Quiz 4:   *Be supposed to.*

Answer the questions in complete sentences, using **be supposed to**.

1. What is a good student supposed to do?

   _____ *A good student is supposed to come to class on time.* ___OR___ _____

   _____ *A good student is always supposed to do his or her homework.* _____

2. If you cut yourself with a knife, what are you supposed to do?

   _____

3. If you lose your credit card, what are you supposed to do?

   _____

4. When you leave the house, what are you supposed to do?

   _____

5. When you finish a candy bar, what are you not supposed to do?

   _____

6. When you have a job interview, what are you supposed to wear?

   _____

7. If you borrow your brother's radio, what are you supposed to do?

   _____

8. If you are sitting down on a crowded bus and an old man gets on, what are you
   supposed to do?

   _____

9. If you go to the beach, what are you supposed to take?

   _____

10. If you need to leave class early, what are you supposed to do?

    _____

11. If you are introduced to a stranger, what are you supposed to say?

    _____

■ **Quiz 5:**   Making suggestions.

Complete the sentences with a form of *let's*, *why don't*, or *could*.

1. **A:** What should we do this weekend?

    B: It's very nice outside. _____*Why don't*_____ we go for a walk in the woods?

2. **A:** I'm falling asleep, and I have another class in five minutes.

    B: _____ you get a cup of coffee?

3. **A:** Which movie should we see tonight?

    B: _____ see *The Great Train Robbery*. I've been wanting to see it for two months.

4. **A:** I'm bored.

    B: You _____ read a good book, or you _____ go outside and play for a while.

5. **A:** I have the most terrible headache, but I have to finish this project before 5 P.M.

    B: _____ you take two aspirin and lie down for ten minutes. Maybe it will get better.

6. **A:** I'm glad our plane arrived on time. How are we going to get to the hotel?

    B: We _____ take a taxi, but that's a little expensive. There's also an airport bus and the local train system.

    A: _____ see what the train schedule is like. If we have a long wait, we can take the bus instead.

7. **A:** I can't decide which camera to buy. They both have many features, but I can't tell which one will work better for me.

    B: There's a 30-day return policy, so you _____ buy one of them, and if you're unhappy with it, just bring it back and buy the other one.

    A: Good idea.

8. **A:** Everyone's using a computer these days. I need to catch up if I want to stay competitive in the job market. What can I do?

   B: You _____ take classes at a private business school or use those videotape lessons. However, I think the best idea is to take a class at the community college first. You should make sure you like computers before you spend a lot of money.

9. **A:** This closet is just full of junk. If I could clear it out, I'd have more room for important things.

   B: _____ I help you? If we work together, we can get it done more quickly, and it'll be fun to talk together.

■ CHAPTER 9 TEST

A. Answer the question(s) at the end of each paragraph. Use a modal verb.

1. You need to write a paper for your English class. You want to find some information on the country of Eritrea, but you don't know which book you need. You find a librarian. What do you say to her?

   _____ *Could you help me find a book about Eritrea?* _____

2. You are going out for the evening with your spouse. A babysitter will look after your children. Before you leave, you give the children some rules of behavior. What do you tell them to do?

   _____

   _____

3. You and your friend Jimmy are walking to class. You have a test today, but Jimmy doesn't feel well. He was up all night coughing, and he slept very little. Jimmy is clearly not well enough to take a test. What do you tell him to do?

   _____

   _____

4. Jimmy didn't listen to you and took the test, even though he didn't feel well. He coughed a lot during the test, and the next week, three other students had bad coughs. When Jimmy got his test back, he had a very low score. What is one thing Jimmy should have done? What is one thing Jimmy should not have done?

   _____

   _____

5. Your friend Pam is getting ready for her first day on her first job. She is not sure what to do. You tell her what most bosses expect of their employees. What are two things that you tell her?

   _____

   _____

6. You are finally retired from your job after working all your life. Elena is having lunch with you, and she asks about your retirement. You tell her how much your life has changed. What are two things that you had to do before that you don't have to do anymore?

   _____

   _____

7. Your cousin Donna is going to visit some friends in Los Angeles, California. She has never been there. Her friends will be busy two of the days while she is there, and she doesn't know what to do during those two days. What are two suggestions that you give her?

_____

_____

B. Complete the dialogues with modal verbs.

1. **A:** I'm so tired! I'm really happy that tomorrow is a holiday and I

___*don't have to*___ go to work. I can sleep late.

B: Not me. We took last Friday off, so I still _____ go to work tomorrow.

A: I'm planning to go downtown and do a little shopping. I also have some errands to run.

B: Speaking of errands, _____ you pick up some stamps for me at the post office?

A: No problem. I _____ mail a package, so I can do both things at

the same time. I _____ pay my bills tonight, too, so that I can mail

them at the post office tomorrow. I _____ mailed them last week, but I was too busy.

B: What are you doing tomorrow evening?

A: I don't have any plans. Why?

B: I was thinking that I could leave work a little early, and we _____ do something together.

A: _____ we go out to dinner and then to a movie?

B: That would be really fun. What do you want to see?

A: _____ see *Secrets of the Dark Woods*. I hear that it's good and scary.

B: Sounds great. If I meet you at the theater, _____ you drive me home? I'll probably go directly to the theater from work.

A: No problem. Well, I _____ go and pay those bills now. See you tomorrow.

B: Bye.

2. **A:** _____ you help me lift this box?

B: Wow! It's heavy. What's in it?

A: My old records. I don't have a record player anymore, and I _____ make some room for my CDs, so I'm putting the LPs in the garage.

B: You _____ sell them. They'll just gather dust in the garage.

A: Who would buy them?

B: There's a used music store on 24th Street. _____ take your records there and see if they'll buy them?

A: They're awfully heavy. _____ you drive me down there in your car?

B: No problem, but I _____ be at my parents' house for dinner in fifteen minutes, so if you want to go, we _____ go now.

A: Great. I just _____ get my house keys, and we can leave. _____ you carry the box out to the car?

B: Sure. Oh. Before we go, _____ if I call my parents? I'm going to tell them I'll be a little late.

A: The phone is in the living room. Help yourself.

CHAPTER 10
Modals, Part 2

■ **Quiz 1:**   Degrees of certainty: present time affirmative and negative.

Complete each sentence with a modal verb to show degree of certainty and make the sentence clear.

1. It is really hot in here. It _____*must be*_____ over 90 degrees. It feels like an oven.

2. I can't believe that anyone would be calling this late at night. It

   _____ my mother. She said that she would call, but it's so late.

3. Hey! This jacket doesn't fit me. It _____ my jacket. All these black jackets look the same.

4. **A:** No one is answering the telephone. Didn't Jeff say that he was going to be home?

   B: He _____ asleep. After all, he starts work at 4 A.M.

5. Mrs. Chu said that she _____ absent from class tonight. Her son is having a fancy dinner, and she is invited.

6. Mrs. White is always complaining about her apartment, her husband, her children,

   and her life. She is a very sad woman. She _____ very unhappy.

7. The doctor listened to the heartbeat in Gina's womb and said that it was very

   strong. In fact, it was so noisy that he thought that it _____ twins.

8. George just bought a new car, and now he always says that he has no money. He

   has a very good salary, so his new car _____ very expensive.

9. **A:** Wow! This is a really large package. What did you order?

   B: I ordered a crystal bowl for my niece for her wedding.

   A: It _____ very fragile. It has a lot of packing material.

10. **A:** I can't find my gray shirt anywhere. I wore it on Monday.

B: I probably thought it was dirty. It _____ in the laundry hamper.

■ **Quiz 2:**   **Degrees of certainty: past time.**

Write a sentence about each paragraph, using the word in parentheses.

1. John is a very conscientious student. He always comes to class, and if he has to be absent, he always tells the teacher. He didn't come to class today, and he didn't call the teacher. Why was John absent?

   a. *(may)* _____ *John may have had a car accident.* _____

   Mary, John's friend, is in the hall. She's not worried about John. She says that John's car is old and is always having problems.

   b. *(must)* _____ *John must have had car trouble.* _____

2. Paula is very upset. She can't find her purse anywhere. This morning she went to the cafeteria and then to her physics class. She also stopped to see her counselor. What happened to Paula's purse?

   a. *(may)* _____

   _____

   b. *(might)* _____

   _____

   Paula's cellular phone rings. It's her mother. After the phone call, Paula is no longer upset, but she needs to go back home.

   c. *(must)* _____

3. Marie looked really terrible after lunch, and she went home shortly thereafter. What happened?

   a. *(may)* _____

   Several people who ate the lasagna in the cafeteria for lunch didn't feel well afterward. Marie ate the lasagna for lunch. What happened?

   b. *(must)* _____

■ Quiz 3:   Degrees of certainty: future time.

Using the information about each situation, complete the sentences.

1. *Situation:*   The students are taking a two-page quiz. There are five minutes left for the quiz. Who will finish the quiz?

   Information: The last two questions on **Ron's** paper are still blank.
   Sally is working on the last question.
   Janet is still working on the first page of the quiz.

   a. _____*Janet*_____ won't finish the quiz.

   b. _____*Ron*_____ might finish the quiz.

   c. _____*Sally*_____ should finish the quiz.

2. *Situation:*   People are running in a 26-mile marathon. Who will finish the marathon?

   Information: **Mark** is in very good shape and has already run in two marathons this year.
   Jane has never run a marathon before, and she trained for only two weeks.
   Martha has never run a marathon before, but she has been training for three months.

   a. _____ might not finish the marathon.

   b. _____ could finish the marathon.

   c. _____ ought to finish the marathon.

3. *Situation:*   We are at the airport in Chicago. Whose flight will arrive on time?

   Information: **Alice's** plane left on time and has had no problems in the air.
   Kay's plane had a mechanical problem and left an hour late.
   Jack's plane left fifteen minutes late, but a strong tail wind helped the plane go faster.

   a. _____ should arrive on time.

   b. _____ won't arrive on time.

   c. _____ might arrive on time.

4. *Situation:*   Several people were interviewed for a job. Who will get the job?

   Information: **Mr. Anton** answered all the questions well, and he is well qualified for the position.
   Mrs. Chu answered the questions well, but she lacks some job qualifications.
   Ms. Callahan was extremely nervous and did not make a good impression.

   a. _____ won't get the job.

   b. _____ should get the job.

   c. _____ may get the job.

■ Quiz 4: Progressive forms of modals.

Complete the sentences, using the appropriate forms of ***must, should,*** or
may/might/could.

1. **A:** Stewardess, are we going to take off soon?

   B: Yes, sir. There was a small problem, but it has been fixed. We
   _____*should be taking off*_____ momentarily.

2. **A:** Should I pack my umbrella?

   B: I checked the weather report, and it wasn't good. When we get there, it
   _____.

3. **A:** Oh, my! This month's water bill is over $100! Last month it was less than $25.

   B: Water _____ somewhere. We'd better call a plumber.

4. **A:** Johnny, why are you watching TV? Your room is a mess, and you
   _____ your room right now.

   B: All right, Mom. I'm going!

5. **A:** Excuse me. I'm looking for the Investment Seminar. It's supposed to be in
   Room 4301.

   B: If it's not in 4301, they _____ in Room 2301. Let me
   check for you.

6. **A:** That's the third time this week that I've seen you looking in the job section of the
   newspaper. You _____ for a new job.

   B: You're right. My new boss and I aren't getting along, so it looks like it's time for
   me to go elsewhere.

7. **A:** Peter has been awfully quiet for more than an hour. What's he doing?

   B: He _____ a computer game, or he
   _____ a comic book. He gets really absorbed in both of
   those things.

8. **A:** I haven't seen Kelly all night. What's she doing?

 B: She _____. She told me that she has two exams tomorrow.

9. **A:** I can't believe it's really 11:30 P.M. It's been so nice visiting with you, but we _____.

 B: And I _____ to bed. I have to get up at 6:30 tomorrow morning. Good night!

■ Quiz 5: Ability.

Answer the questions in complete sentences. Use **can** or **could**.

1. What is something a teacher can do but a student can't?

 _____*A teacher can assign homework, but a student can't.*_____

2. What is something that you can do in a movie theater but you can't do in class?

 _____

 _____

3. What is something that a bus passenger can do but a car driver can't?

 _____

 _____

4. What was something that you couldn't do as a child but you can do now?

 _____

 _____

5. What is something that a cat can do but a dog can't?

 _____

 _____

6. What is something that you can do with a computer but you can't do with a typewriter?

 _____

 _____

■ **Quiz 6:** Repeated action in the past.

Rewrite each sentence using **would**, if possible. If not possible, write **no change**.

1. I used to ride my bike to work when I lived in Taylorville.

   I would ride my bike to work when I lived in Taylorville.

   _____

2. Mary used to ride her bike to work until it got too dangerous.

   _____

   _____

3. When my Uncle Stanley was alive, he used to take us children for rides in his convertible.

   _____

   _____

4. Tom used to use his brother's old typewriter, but now he has a computer.

   _____

5. Every night when my dad got home from work, he used to sit down in his armchair, read the newspaper for five minutes, and fall asleep.

   _____

   _____

6. Before Dennis took the spelling improvement class, he always used to lose points on his assignments because of poor spelling.

   _____

   _____

7. Jake used to be late for class every morning because he had a job on the night shift.

   _____

   _____

8. My grandmother used to work in her garden every day until she developed arthritis in her knees.

   _____

   _____

9. I used to study at the University of Wisconsin before I transferred to the University of Illinois.

_____

_____

10. Alex used to work for IBM, but now he is working for Apple Computer.

_____

_____

11. Lisa used to be able to speak Chinese, but she can't anymore.

_____

_____

■ Quiz 7: *Would rather.*

Use **would rather** and the given words to write a sentence.

1. *(stay home, last night)*
    <u>I would rather have stayed home last night.</u>

2. *(chicken, fish, dinner)*

_____

3. *(give, not, today)*

_____

4. *(listen, watch, right now)*

_____

5. *(beach, Disneyland, on vacation)*

_____

6. *(do better, next quiz)*

_____

7. *(roses, fruit trees)*

_____

8. *(cook, not, tonight)*

_____

9. *(New York, San Francisco)*

_____

10. *(drive, take)*

_____

11. *(carrots, raw, cooked)*

_____

■ CHAPTER 10 TEST

A. Using the information about each situation, complete the sentences.

1. *Situation:* The students took a difficult quiz. This is how far they had gotten five minutes before the end of the quiz. Who finished the quiz?

   Information: The last two questions on **Ron's** paper were still blank.
   Sally was working on the last question.
   Janet had not finished one of the questions on page one, but I think she had finished the other page.

   a. Ron _____*may/might/could have finished*_____ the quiz.

   b. Sally _____*must have finished*_____ the quiz.

   c. Janet _____*might not have finished*_____ the quiz.

2. *Situation:* Jean made some phone calls to her friends at 7:30 P.M., but no one answered. What were her friends doing?

   Information: **Jeff** is usually at the library every evening from 7:00 P.M. to 9:00 P.M.
   Eva usually eats dinner at 7:30 P.M., and sometimes she doesn't answer the telephone.
   When **Jack** is at home, he always answers the telephone.

   a. Jeff _____ at home.

   b. Eva _____ at home.

   c. Jack _____ at home.

3. *Situation:* Mrs. Chang is in the kitchen. Her husband and three children are at home. She hears water running. Who is taking a shower?

   Information: **Mr. Chang** often takes a shower after work, but Mrs. Chang hears someone working in the garage.
   Her son **Tom** had a basketball game that afternoon, and when he got home, he was very sweaty.
   Her daughter, **Julie**, only takes a shower in the morning.
   Her other son, **Kevin**, was working in the garden earlier, and she thinks he is still outside.

   a. Mr. Chang _____ a shower.

   b. Kevin _____ a shower.

   c. Julie _____ a shower.

   d. Tom _____ a shower.

4. *Situation:*   Mr. Anton loves to read, and his friends often give him recommendations. Which books did Mr. Anton read?

   Information: **Ms. Adams** recommended *Trials by Night*. Mr. Anton has enjoyed all of the books Ms. Adams has recommended.
   Mr. French recommended *The Terrible War*. Mr. Anton has enjoyed one or two of the books Mr. French has recommended.
   Mrs. White recommended *The Thinking Mystery*. Mr. Anton has never enjoyed any of her recommendations, but she is a very close friend.

   a. Mr. Anton _____ the book Ms. Adams recommended.

   b. Mr. Anton _____ the book Mr. French recommended.

   c. Mr. Anton _____ the book Mrs. White recommended.

B. Complete the sentences, using an appropriate modal verb.

1. I really _____*should study*_____ for the test tomorrow, but I

   _____*would rather go*_____ to a movie with you.

2. I haven't been outside since I came to work, but it _____

   hard because everyone is carrying a wet umbrella. I _____
   an umbrella, but I didn't hear the weather forecast. Now I'm sure to get wet on the
   way home.

3. When we were kids, my parents _____ us to Disneyland

   every summer. I don't need to go there again. I _____
   New York City than go to Los Angeles again.

4. If I _____ my work early, I _____
   to meet you for the 6:00 movie. I'll give you a call you and let you know.

5. Ten years ago, I _____ to work in just 10 minutes. Now

   the traffic is so bad that I _____ to work in less than
   40 minutes. Sometimes, it even takes an hour!

6. Those two people look so similar that they _____ closely
   related. I think Julie told me they are first cousins.

7. **A:** Wow! You are almost 30 minutes late. The traffic _____
   terrible!
   B: It was. A terrible accident at Zanker Road was blocking three lanes. The traffic
   was barely moving.

8. **A:** If I _____ my reservation, I would like to leave on an earlier flight. Right now I'm booked on the 6 P.M. flight.

   B: There _____ plenty of room on the 4:30 flight. Saturday afternoons are usually pretty light. Let me check for you.

9. When I was a kid, I was really skinny. The other kids _____ me and laugh at me, so I started lifting weights. No one laughs at me anymore.

10. I'm afraid that I _____ you more than five minutes, Mr. Green. I'm very busy, and I _____ an important meeting at 3 P.M.

11. I _____ to a movie with you last night instead of babysitting. I don't know why I told Mrs. Ramirez that I would do it. I

   _____ crazy.

CHAPTER 11
The Passive

■ **Quiz 1:** Forming the passive.

A. Change the active to the passive.

1. A speeding truck hit my car.

   _____ *My car was hit by a speeding truck.* _____

2. The children have cleaned the house.

   _____

3. The waitress is going to bring your drink very soon.

   _____

4. Mary is taking care of Alex's son.

   _____

5. The students write many papers during the semester.

   _____

6. My little sister broke the flower vase in the hall.

   _____

B. Change the active to the passive if possible. If a change is not possible, write *no change*.

1. A large meteor killed all the dinosaurs on earth.

   All the dinosaurs on earth were killed by a large meteor.

2. Did an earthquake damage the office building?

   _____

3. Kathy is working in her kitchen.

   _____

4. Alice has interviewed more than forty people for this job.

   _____

5. Shirley saw some Persian horses at the zoo.

   _____

6. Are the students unhappy with the test results?

   _____

7. The committee is looking for a solution to the problem.

   _____

8. Will the electric company raise our rates next month?

   _____

9. Barbara has been teaching history for twelve years.

   _____

10. Will their plan succeed?

    _____

11. Hurricane Irene is going to hit the East Coast by tomorrow night.

    _____

■ **Quiz 2:** Using the passive with and without the *by*-phrase.

Change the active sentences to passive sentences if possible. Keep the same tense. Include the *by*-phrase only if necessary.

1. Something killed all the dinosaurs millions of years ago.

   All the dinosaurs were killed millions of years ago.

2. The results of the tests greatly pleased the students.

   _____

3. Jackie is going to translate the report from English to Russian.

   _____

4. The mail carrier left three packages in my office.

   _____

5. A terrible accident occurred at the corner of Main Street and 22nd Avenue.

   _____

6. When did someone build the first personal computer?

   _____

7. Millions of people watch the World Cup soccer game on TV every year.

   _____

8. Someone performed several pieces by Bach in the school auditorium last Friday.

   _____

9. Jim's plane landed safely after a very bumpy flight.

   _____

10. Construction workers will finish Highway 92 before winter.

   _____

11. Professor Brown is going to write a new grammar book during summer vacation.

   _____

■ **Quiz 3:** Indirect objects as passive subjects.

A. Find the indirect object in each sentence and make it the focus of attention by using it as the subject of a passive sentence.

1. Professor Rivers gives the students homework only at the end of the class.

   The students are given homework by Professor Rivers only at the end of the

   class. (indirect object = the students)

2. Some company will send me the refund within 60 days.

   _____

   _____

3. Someone will pay the translator $10 for each page of the document.

   _____

   _____

4. Dr. Ikeda is showing the businessmen the new computer chip.

   _____

   _____

5. The bank didn't lend Tom the money for a new car.

   _____

   _____

6. A friend took Ann a casserole because Ann was sick at home.

   _____

   _____

B. Rewrite each sentence in Part **A.** Make the direct object the focus of attention by using it as the subject of a passive sentence.

1. Professor Rivers gives the students homework only at the end of the class.

   Homework is given by Professor Rivers (to the students) only at the end of the

   class. (direct object = homework)

2. Some company will send me the refund within 60 days.

   _____

   _____

3. Someone will pay the translator $10 for each page of the document.

   _____

   _____

4. Dr. Ikeda is showing the businessmen the new computer chip.

   _____

   _____

5. The bank didn't lend Tom the money for a new car.

   _____

   _____

6. A friend took Ann a casserole because Ann was sick at home.

   _____

   _____

■ **Quiz 4:** The passive form of modals and phrasal modals.

Complete the sentences with the given words, active or passive. Use the correct tense.

1. James *(should + tell)* ____should be told____ the truth about the company's financial situation.

2. More than 200 people *(may + kill)* _____ in the train accident.

3. Your teeth *(must + check)* _____ regularly in order to avoid cavities.

4. People *(ought to + not + fire)* _____ from their jobs because of their age.

5. Your homework *(have to + finish)* _____ before the next class session.

6. This unusual species of fish *(can't + identify)* _____ by scientists.

7. We *(should + sit)* _____ down because the interview is going to begin.

8. This conversation group is too large, so it *(should + split)* _____ into two smaller groups.

9. According to the fire chief, the fire *(must + start)* _____ by a cigarette.

10. My refrigerator *(had better + fix)* _____ soon, or I will complain to the building manager.

11. Roberto *(may + give)* _____ harder exercises by his teacher because he already understands these mathematical ideas completely.

■ **Quiz 5:** **Stative passive verbs + prepositions.**
Complete the sentences with your own words. Supply the correct prepositions.

1. I am worried . . .

    _____ I am worried about the next test. _____

2. The person next to me is dressed . . .

    _____

3. I am not interested . . .

    _____

4. One of my friends is terrified . . .

    _____

5. During the holidays, stores are crowded . . .

    _____

6. My classmates are prepared . . .

    _____

7. London is located . . .

    _____

8. A complete sentence is composed . . .

    _____

9. I am excited . . .

    _____

10. All of the students are accustomed . . .

    _____

11. Are you done . . .

    _____

■ **Quiz 6:** *Get* + passive.

A. Choose the phrase that best completes each sentence.

1. __*d*__ I am getting sleepy, so

2. _____ I was late to Ed's party because

3. _____ Although I packed my shirts very carefully,

4. _____ Sam is going to get dressed after

5. _____ Maria got sick last week, and

6. _____ If the children get bored,

7. _____ I got sleepy while driving my car, so

8. _____ I might be late to Ed's party if

9. _____ I am very excited about our vacation, and

10. _____ Chris is going to get mad at you if

11. _____ My dog gets bored at home alone all day, so

a. I got lost and couldn't find his house.

b. you don't hurry up and get dressed.

c. I stopped at a restaurant and had some coffee.

d. I had better go to bed.

e. they might get wrinkled in my suitcase.

f. my meeting doesn't get done on time.

g. I'm worried that I might forget to pack something.

h. he takes a shower.

i. I often take him to the park.

j. she still hasn't gotten well.

k. you can take them to the park.

B. Complete the sentences with an appropriate form of *get* and the given verbs. Use the correct tense.

Mary: John! It's good to see you again. I heard that you were sick.

John: Yes. I *(sick)* ____*got sick*____ last Wednesday, and I missed four days of work.

Mary: How do you feel now?

John: I *(better)* _____, but I still *(chilly)* _____ even when the heat is on. I guess I'm not completely well yet.

Mary: Are you behind on your work?

John: I was lucky. I was able to take a lot of work home with me, so all my work *(done)* _____. I knew I had to keep up because it *(busy)* _____ around the office lately.

Mary: If business continues to improve, we all might *(rich)* _____ soon!

John: That would be wonderful. When I *(old)* _____, I want to have saved enough money for my retirement.

Mary: Oh! It *(late)* _____. I need to go to another meeting, and I need to *(prepare)* _____. See you later, and *(well)* _____!

John: Thanks, Mary. If you *(bored)* _____, you can dream about being rich.

■ Quiz 7: **Participial adjectives.**

Decide if the adjective in *italics* is used correctly. If it is incorrect, correct the error.

1. Yesterday, a group of friends and I went to a *depressed* basketball game.
   depressing

2. We were very *surprising* because not many people were there.

3. At first, the teams played well, and it was *thrilling* to watch them.

4. Jim got so *exciting* that he jumped out of his seat.

5. It was *embarrassed* because he spilled his soda on the lady in front of him.

6. She was quite *annoyed* and got mad at Jim.

7. We were *shocking* when our favorite player fell and had to leave the game.

8. Without him, it was very *frustrated* because our team couldn't score any points.

9. It was very *disappointing* for us to watch our team lose.

10. We were very *confusing* because the lady in front of us was smiling.

11. Then we found out that she felt very *satisfied* because she supported the other team.

■ CHAPTER 11 TEST

A. Most of the sentences in the paragraphs are in active voice. Six of the sentences would be better in the passive voice. Find the six sentences and rewrite them in the passive. When making your choice, think about focus and the importance of subjects.

Thanksgiving

(1) Americans celebrate Thanksgiving on the fourth Thursday in November. (2) People close schools and many businesses on Thanksgiving Day and the day after. (3) Thanksgiving usually marks the beginning of the holiday season. (4) It is traditional for Macy's department store to hold an annual Thanksgiving Day Parade in New York City. (5) Stores are crowded with people who are ready to begin their holiday shopping. (6) People may decorate stores, homes, and classrooms with turkeys, dried leaves, and pumpkins. (7) For some people, the highlight of the weekend is high school, college, and professional football games. (8) On this day, all people are thankful for the many good things in their lives. (9) Food is an important part of the Thanksgiving Day celebration. (10) A traditional Thanksgiving meal includes turkey, cranberry sauce, and pumpkin pie.

(11) People held the first Thanksgiving Day in 1621. (12) A group of people, the Pilgrims, came from England to find religious freedom. (13) Nearby Indians worked with the Pilgrims through the first harsh winter and the first harvest. (14) Then, the Indians and the Pilgrims celebrated together. (15) People easily hunted wild turkeys in the nearby forests, and they became the traditional main course at the Thanksgiving feast. (16) Congress made Thanksgiving a legal holiday in 1941.

1. _____*Thanksgiving is celebrated by Americans on the fourth Thursday in November.*_____

2. _____

_____

3. _____

_____

4. _____

_____

5. _____

_____

6. _____

_____

B. Change the active to the passive.

1. The school gave scholarships to many students from low-income families.

   _____Scholarships were given to many students from low-income families._____

2. A falling pine cone hit Michael on the head.

   _____

   _____

3. People check the machinery five times before they put it in a box for shipping.

   _____

   _____

4. Someone is going to cut down the weeds on the hill.

   _____

   _____

5. An anonymous donor gave the Cancer Foundation $2 million.

   _____

   _____

6. Everybody should obey all signs and placards.

   _____

   _____

7. Someone may tow your car if you park in this area.

   _____

   _____

8. The museum loaned the old book to the university.

   _____

   _____

Midterm Exam

Choose the best answer to complete each sentence. Write the letter of the answer in the space.

Example: John ___c___ read a book quietly in his room than play tennis with his brother.

    a. prefer   c. would rather

    b. had better   d. had to

1. Bruce was twenty minutes late for this morning's meeting. He _____ stuck in traffic.

    a. might be   c. had to be

    b. must be   d. must have been

2. The teacher was surprised that the students needed more time. They _____ finish the quiz in 30 minutes.

    a. should have could   c. should be can

    b. should have been able to   d. had better

3. When the movie actress entered the room, everyone turned and looked at _____.

    a. herself   c. her

    b. she   d. hers

4. Dogs make excellent pets. _____ provide good companionship and even protection.

    a. They   c. It

    b. Its   d. It's

5. By the time Brian _____ a parking space, he was late for the movie.

    a. was finding   c. had found

    b. was found   d. finds

6. Spring is Mrs. Mojadedi's favorite season because flowers _____ everywhere.

    a. appear   c. will appear

    b. are appearing   d. are going to appear

7. Shirley wasn't able to concentrate all morning because she _____ at all the night before.

   a. wasn't sleeping

   b. hadn't slept

   c. sleeps

   d. hasn't been sleeping

8. Peter rarely _____ a promotion at work because he never does more than he has to.

   a. got

   b. is getting

   c. will get

   d. gets

9. Mrs. Taylor is worried because the children _____ be home two hours ago.

   a. have got to

   b. ought to

   c. were supposed to

   d. didn't have to

10. _____ please answer the telephone? I'm washing the dishes, and my hands are all wet.

    a. Would you

    b. Would you mind

    c. May you

    d. You must

11. Can I borrow _____? I must have left mine at home.

    a. one of your pen

    b. one of your pens

    c. one your pen

    d. one your pens

12. Maria has invited all of the students and all of the _____ parents to her birthday party.

    a. students'

    b. students

    c. student's

    d. students their

13. By the time William is forty years old, he _____ fifteen novels and two collections of short stories.

    a. wrote

    b. will have written

    c. has written

    d. will be writing

14. I'm not sure where Johnny is, but he _____ to music in his room.

    a. might be listening

    b. might listen

    c. might have listened

    d. must have been listening

15. You _____ hungry already! You just ate a big lunch and a dish of ice cream.

    a. must not be

    b. can't be

    c. could have been

    d. might not be

16. _____ not smoking? I'm very allergic to cigarette smoke.

    a. Would you   c. Would you mind

    b. Can you   d. Will you

17. The Chinese _____ the oldest calendar of any culture in the world today.

    a. have had   c. have

    b. has had   d. has

18. Each of _____ graduated from school and found a good job.

    a. their children have   c. their children has

    b. their child has   d. their childrens have

19. Mario _____ for four hours straight. He had better take a break to stretch and eat something.

    a. is studying   c. studied

    b. was studying   d. has been studying

20. Janice _____ a koala bear before she went to Australia last November.

    a. had never seen   c. had ever seen

    b. has never seen   d. doesn't see

21. The employees at ABC Motor Company get paid _____ week.

    a. every other   c. one after the other

    b. each other   d. another

22. It looks like your cup is empty. Would you like _____ cup of coffee?

    a. other   c. one another

    b. another   d. the other

23. Babies like to talk to _____ in order to practice the sounds of a language.

    a. itself   c. itselves

    b. themself   d. themselves

24. Oh no! _____ is missing! We'll need to call the police.

    a. All of the stamps   c. All of the computers

    b. All of the jewelry   d. All of the children

25. _____ a different topic. We will study Chapters 1 through 10 this semester.

    a. Each of the chapter covers   c. Each of the chapters covers

    b. Each of the chapters cover   d. All of the chapter cover

26. I don't think we'll need an umbrella this afternoon. The forecast is for _____ late tonight.

    a. a little rain   c. a few rain

    b. little rain   d. few rain

27. This chemical is very dangerous. You _____ handle it without gloves and goggles.

    a. don't have to   c. had better

    b. have to   d. must not

28. Philip usually doesn't take a shower while his wife _____ the laundry.

    a. will do   c. is going to do

    b. is doing   d. was doing

29. I'm amazed! None of my workers _____ any problems with their equipment since we bought it.

    a. have   c. have had

    b. has   d. has had

30. One hour may be enough for the midterm, but two hours _____ necessary for the final exam.

    a. was   c. is

    b. were   d. are

31. Until I _____ a house and a good job, I am not planning to get married and start a family.

    a. have   c. am having

    b. will have   d. am going to have

32. While the children are watching a movie later this afternoon, I _____ a nap.

    a. am taking   c. was taking

    b. take   d. will be taking

33. Whenever people _____ this memorial, they will remember the soldiers who died for their country.

    a. saw   c. are seeing

    b. see   d. will see

34. After the hurricane has passed, people _____ to their homes to check on the damage.

    a. will be able to return   c. will have returned

    b. could have returned   d. return

35. The suspect will not talk to the police until his lawyer _____ present.

    a. was
    b. is going to be
    c. will have been
    d. is

36. The students _____ go to school on Monday because it is a holiday.

    a. doesn't have to
    b. don't have to
    c. didn't
    d. must not

37. If you have no plans for this afternoon, we _____ see a movie or do some shopping.

    a. should
    b. would
    c. could
    d. must

38. By this December, we _____ in this house for more than thirty years.

    a. will live
    b. had lived
    c. will have been living
    d. are going to be living

39. When Kevin went to the refrigerator for a snack, _____ many things to eat.

    a. there isn't
    b. there aren't
    c. there wasn't
    d. there weren't

40. Please don't disturb me right now. I _____ to finish the last page of this report.

    a. try
    b. am trying
    c. will try
    d. have tried

41. Sally isn't sure, but she _____ her purse in the restaurant.

    a. might leave
    b. might have been left
    c. might have left
    d. might be leaving

42. High blood pressure _____ by medication.

    a. can control
    b. has controlled
    c. can be controlling
    d. can be controlled

43. If a person _____ one foreign language, it is usually easier to learn a second one.

    a. has studied
    b. will study
    c. was studied
    d. studied

44. Don't worry. All of the reports _____ by the time you get here tomorrow morning.

    a. will complete
    b. will be completed
    c. are completed
    d. have been completed

45. These coffee beans _____ in the mountains of Colombia.

    a. were handpicked

    b. handpicked

    c. were handpicked by someone

    d. were handpicking

46. I'm sorry, but Room 1102 is not available. It _____ by another group.

    a. was using

    b. was being used

    c. is using

    d. is being used

47. Kevin didn't finish watching the movie because it _____.

    a. was bored

    b. was being bored

    c. was being boring

    d. was boring

48. You had better throw that meat away. I'm sure that it _____.

    a. is spoiling

    b. is spoiled

    c. is being spoiled

    d. spoils

49. The neighbors are very much _____ a homeless shelter in their area.

    a. opposed to

    b. opposing to

    c. opposed about

    d. opposing about

50. Mr. Patterson _____ from his job because his firm was bought out by another company.

    a. was firing

    b. fired

    c. got fired

    d. gets fired

CHAPTER 12
Noun Clauses

■ **Quiz 1:** Noun clauses beginning with a question word.

Change the question in parentheses to a noun clause. Pay attention to sentence punctuation.

1. (How did the fire start?) Investigators are trying to find out . . .

    _____*Investigators are trying to find out how the fire started.*_____

2. (When does Flight 2803 arrive?) The timetable can tell you . . .

    _____

3. (Who ate the last piece of pie?) My little sister wants to know . . .

    _____

4. (When does the next train leave?) Do you know . . .

    _____

5. (What grade did I get on the last quiz?) I wonder . . .

    _____

6. (How often do you go to the gym?) I would like to know . . .

    _____

7. (What time does the meeting start?) Let's ask him . . .

    _____

8. (Which bus goes to the courthouse?) Could you tell me . . .

    _____

9. (Where is the nearest mailbox?) Do you know . . .

    _____

10. (Where did she go after the meeting?) I don't know . . .

    _____

11. (What color sweater would Jim like?) I wonder . . .

    _____

■ **Quiz 2:** Noun clauses beginning with *whether* or *if.*

Change the question in parentheses to a noun clause. Pay attention to sentence punctuation.

1. (Has the forest fire been extinguished yet?) Please tell me . . .

   Please tell me whether the forest fire has been extinguished. OR
   Please tell me if the forest fire has been extinguished. OR
   Please tell me whether or not the forest fire has been extinguished.

2. (Will Flight 2803 arrive on time?) Do you know . . .

   _____

3. (Is there any pie left?) My little sister wants to know . . .

   _____

4. (Does the next train go to Union City?) I wonder . . .

   _____

5. (Are you happy with your grade on the last quiz?) I would like to know . . .

   _____

6. (Does Tom go to the gym every afternoon?) Can you tell me . . .

   _____

7. (Do her meetings usually end on time?) Please tell me . . .

   _____

8. (Does this bus go by the courthouse?) Do you know . . .

   _____

9. (Has the mail already been picked up?) I would like to know . . .

   _____

10. (Did Ruth stay after school for the meeting?) I don't know . . .

    _____

11. (Would Jim prefer a sweater or a shirt?) I wonder . . .

    _____

■ **Quiz 3:** **Question words followed by infinitives.**

Complete the sentences, using infinitives in your completions.

1. I was completely lost. I didn't know which way ____*to go*____ or whom

_____ .

2. The supervisor gave me terrible directions. I couldn't decide what

_____ or even how _____ .

3. Mr. Lee can't decide whether _____ or to visit his family
during the holidays.

4. I've told you everything I know about the crime. I don't know what else

_____ .

5. The teacher gave us very clear directions for our essay. He told us how many words

_____ , what color pen _____ , and when

_____ .

6. The patient asked the doctor how often _____ .

7. Alex has two girlfriends. He can't decide which one _____ to the
school dance.

■ **Quiz 4:** Noun clauses beginning with *that*.

A. For each sentence, show another way that the sentence can be written. The sentence should contain a noun clause.

1. That Don isn't feeling well should be obvious.

   It should be obvious that Don isn't feeling well.

2. It is unfortunate that Sally won't be able to attend the ceremony.

   _____

3. That the doctor gave you the wrong prescription is unlikely.

   _____

4. That the little girl survived the plane crash is a miracle.

   _____

5. It surprises me that Rosa didn't finish the project on time.

   _____

6. It is clear that no one will pass this class without additional help from the teacher.

   _____

B. Complete the sentences with your own ideas by using *that*-clauses.

1. I'm pleased . . .

   I'm pleased that I got a good grade on my last quiz.

2. I'm disappointed . . .

   _____

3. I have two problems with my English. One problem is . . . The other problem is . . .

   _____

4. I read about the hurricane in the newspaper. It is unfortunate . . .

   _____

5. When we learn English, it seems to me . . .

   _____

■ **Quiz 5:** **Quoted speech.**

Here is a conversation written in script form. This is what you would see if you were performing in a movie or a play.

Mary is talking to her teacher, Mr. Thomas, about her last quiz.

Mr. Thomas: You didn't do well on the quiz. What happened? You usually do very well on quizzes.

Mary: I really didn't have enough time to study. My mother hasn't been well, and I was taking care of her.

Mr. Thomas: You should have told me! You could have taken the quiz on a different day when you felt more prepared.

Mary: Can I take the quiz again?

Mr. Thomas: I'm afraid that you can take a quiz only once.

Mary: Do you think that this quiz will lower my grade?

Mr. Thomas: Your grades on the first two quizzes are good, so your average isn't too bad. You can make it up on the next two quizzes.

Mary: I'll do my best. Thanks for talking to me.

Here is the same conversation written for a book in quoted speech. Add the necessary punctuation and capitalization.

Mr. Thomas told Mary, "You didn't do very well on the last quiz he asked what happened and said you usually do very well on quizzes

Mary said I really didn't have enough time to study my mother hasn't been well and I was taking care of her

You should have told me Mr. Thomas remarked you could have taken the quiz on a different day when you felt more prepared

Can I take the quiz again asked Mary

I'm afraid that you can take a quiz only once answered Mr. Thomas

Mary inquired do you think that this quiz will lower my grade

Your grades on the first two quizzes were good he commented so your average isn't too bad he added you can make it up on the next two quizzes

I'll do my best Mary responded thanks for talking to me

■ **Quiz 6:** Reported speech: verb forms in noun clauses.

Use the information in the dialogue to complete the sentences in the paragraph. Add the correct word to introduce the noun clause. Put in the correct pronoun. Change the verbs to a past form as appropriate.

Mr. Thomas: You didn't do well on the quiz. What happened? You usually do very well on quizzes.

Mary: I really didn't have enough time to study. My mother hasn't been well, and I was taking care of her.

Mr. Thomas: You should have told me! You could have taken the quiz on a different day when you felt more prepared.

Mary: Can I take the quiz again?

Mr. Thomas: I'm afraid that you can take a quiz only once.

Mary: Do you think that this quiz will lower my grade?

Mr. Thomas: Your grades on the first two quizzes were good, so your average isn't too bad. You can make it up on the next two quizzes.

Mary: I'll do my best. Thanks for talking to me.

Mr. Thomas told Mary _____*that*_____ she _____*hadn't done*_____ well on the last quiz and asked her _____ . Mary answered _____ she _____ enough time to study because her mother hadn't been well, and she _____ taking care of her. Mr. Thomas was surprised and said that she should _____ him. He explained _____ she could _____ the quiz on a different day when she had felt more prepared. Mary wondered _____ she _____ the quiz again. Mr. Thomas apologized and told her _____ she _____ a quiz only once. Mary asked him _____ he thought _____ this quiz _____ her grade. Mr. Thomas responded _____ her grades on the first two quizzes were good, so her average _____ too bad. He added _____ she _____ make it up on the next two quizzes. Mary promised _____ do her best and thanked him for talking to her.

■ **Quiz 7:** Using the subjunctive in noun clauses.

Complete the sentences with your own words.

1. It is essential that we . . . for English class.

    _____*It is essential that we read Chapter 15 for homework for English class.*_____

2. Because Janice was often late to class, the teacher demanded that . . .

    _____

3. For the New Year's Eve party, the invitation requested that . . .

    _____

4. For a job interview, it is imperative that the interviewee . . .

    _____

5. For the school field trip, the teacher asked that the parents . . .

    _____

6. If a person has dangerous cleaning products in his kitchen, it is vital that . . .

    _____

7. In some churches in Europe, they insist that tourists . . .

    _____

8. If sellers want to get a good price for their house, real estate agents recommend that they . . .

    _____

9. If my teenage son wants to stay out past 10 P.M., it is necessary that he . . .

    _____

10. Since we are unable to make a decision at today's meeting, I suggest that we . . .

    _____

11. When Mrs. Robinson had to return to work after twenty years, the job counselor advised that . . .

    _____

■ Quiz 8:   Using *-ever* words.

    A. Change the dependent clause to a noun clause using an *-ever* word.

1. On casual Fridays, employees may wear any style of clothes that they like.

      On casual Fridays, employees may wear whatever they like.

2. The newspaper will publish any of the drawings that win prizes in the school art competition.

    _____

3. Any place that he goes, people enjoy talking to him because he has such a friendly and pleasant manner.

    _____

4. You get the money for me in any way that you can, as long as you get me the money by the first of the month.

    _____

5. The orchestra is ready, and we can start the music at any time that you are ready to begin the program.

    _____

6. The speaker would be glad to talk to anyone who has questions after the lecture.

    _____

    B. Complete the following by using *-ever* words.

1. I will follow you _____*wherever*_____ you go because I have no idea where we are and I don't want to get lost.

2. You should buy _____ jacket pleases you because you are the one who is going to wear it, not me.

3. At the end of the semester, the art students can bring home

    _____ they made in class.

4. Most voters choose _____ candidate promises to give them the most personal benefit.

5. _____ correctly answers the most questions in 30 seconds will get a chance to win the $25,000 prize.

6. I have the whole day free, so _____ long you want to spend working in the garden is fine with me.

■ CHAPTER 12 TEST

A. Complete these sentences with noun clauses. The noun clause must contain the word or phrase in parentheses.

1. The children wonder what . . . *(get)*

   The children wonder what they should get their father for his birthday.

2. Jane is sure that . . . *(turn off)*

   _____

3. Phillip is not sure when . . . *(hand in)*

   _____

4. Susan didn't know what . . . *(buy)*

   _____

5. Do you know if . . . *(leave)*

   _____

6. Rosa's financial advisor recommends that . . . *(invest)*

   _____

7. The Smiths wonder whether . . . *(cancel)*

   _____

8. Brian believes that . . . *(steal)*, but I don't think so.

   _____

9. It is important that each hiker . . . *(bring)*

   _____

10. Do you know how . . . *(fix)*

    _____

11. Ms. Adams insists that . . . *(be)*

    _____

B. Rewrite the quoted sentences as reported speech. Choose the most appropriate speaking word; use formal verb tenses.

Annie and Robert are having coffee the week after final exams.

1. Robert said, "How did your final exams go? Mine were tough."

   _____*Robert asked Annie how her final exams had gone and said that his had*_____

   _____*been tough.*_____

2. Annie said, "My exams went well, but I didn't even have enough time to finish the last question in history class."

   _____

   _____

3. Robert said, "That must have been a tough exam. When will you find out your grades?"

   _____

   _____

4. Annie said, "My teachers usually post them on their office doors on the day after the exam, but I haven't looked yet."

   _____

   _____

5. Robert said, "What are you going to do during vacation? I'll be spending the vacation with my uncle in New York."

   _____

   _____

6. Annie said, "I may drive down to Los Angeles to visit my cousins. After that, I don't know what I'm going to do."

   _____

   _____

CHAPTER *13*
Adjective Clauses

■ **Quiz 1:** Adjective clause pronouns used as subject, object, and object of a preposition; *whose*.

Combine the sentences, using the second sentence as an adjective clause.

1. Sally finally finished typing the letters. The department supervisor needs to sign them.

   Sally finally finished typing the letters that the department supervisor needs

   to sign.

2. The red station wagon was driven by a drunk driver. It caused the accident.

   _____

   _____

3. The police talked to the woman. Her car had been broken into.

   _____

   _____

4. The woman seemed well qualified for the position. Mr. North just interviewed her.

   _____

   _____

5. Mrs. Tanaka is looking for the person. The person's car is blocking her driveway.

   _____

   _____

6. Joe's parents don't like the music. Joe listens to the music.

   _____

   _____

7. My grandmother bought a lot of clothes. The clothes were on sale.

_____

_____

8. The issue is not relevant to our current discussion. Many people are talking about the issue.

_____

_____

9. The printer is fast and dependable. Jason bought it last week.

_____

_____

10. People are in great demand in today's job market. People have advanced computer skills.

_____

_____

11. The principal presented awards to the children. Their artwork was chosen for the citywide art contest.

_____

_____

■ **Quiz 2:** Adjective clause pronouns: *where* and *when.*

Complete the sentences, using **where**, **when,** or **that.** Sometimes more than one choice is possible.

1. Jack would like to know the name of the store _____*where*_____ I got my new DVD player.

2. Philip will meet us at the bus stop _____ is on the corner of 23rd Avenue and Main Street.

3. The travel agent needs to know some alternative dates _____ we can leave on vacation.

4. Can you run upstairs and get my green scarf? It's in the closet _____ I keep my winter coat.

5. The house _____ Maria is going to buy has two bedrooms and one bathroom.

6. The months _____ have 30 days are April, June, September, and November.

7. I remember the time _____ Robert forgot to turn off the bathroom faucet and we came home to a house full of water.

8. When we go to Atlanta, George wants to drive by the house _____ he grew up to see if it still looks the same.

9. The office _____ you are going to be working in is down the hall, the second door to the left.

10. Paul has really enjoyed all of the cities _____ he has visited during his trip through India.

11. The day _____ we got married was probably the happiest day of my life.

■ **Quiz 3:** **Using adjective clauses.**

Complete the sentences with adjective clauses.

1. I've really made a mess of the whole situation. There is no one

   ___*who can help me now*___.

2. Tomorrow is clean-up day. Anyone _____ is welcome to come and help.

3. I'm so pleased to be invited to your party. Is there anything _____?

4. I know that you are looking for a job. The local supermarket is looking for someone

   _____. Maybe you can apply.

5. The tea pots are made in two different sizes. The ones _____

   should go on the top shelf. The ones _____ should go on the

   lower shelf.

6. You are really gaining weight. You should stop eating anything _____.

7. The only one _____ is that one. I really don't like any of the

   others.

8. I think I've included everyone on the guest list. Can you think of anyone

   _____?

9. When choosing a new car, I consider only one _____.

10. Everyone _____ will need to leave their name and address

    on this sheet of paper.

■ **Quiz 4:** Punctuating adjective clauses.

A. Add commas where necessary.

1. I returned the calculator to Minna, who had a difficult math quiz the next day.

2. The supervisor called in the workers whose job performance was less than satisfactory. He gave the other workers the afternoon off.

3. Mrs. Wood would like to find someone who can organize and catalog her collection of Asian art.

4. I have looked everywhere for my grammar book which I am sure I left on the dining table. I can't find it anywhere.

5. Paul will call you at 5:30 P.M. when he will be home from work.

6. Mr. Parker collects toy guns which were manufactured in the 1950s.

7. The roof of my house which is already 20 years old is leaking badly and in need of repair.

8. The hunger program which Jack volunteers for feeds more than 250 families each month.

9. The Red Cross which provides humanitarian aid to victims of wars and natural disasters is the favorite charity of the president's wife.

10. I recently got the autograph of J.K. Rowling who is the author of the Harry Potter series of books.

11. The veterans who fought in World War II were honored at a luncheon at the Commonwealth Club.

B. Circle the correct explanation of the meaning of each sentence.

1. The sales clerk put the sweaters which were on sale in the display window.
    a. *All* the sweaters in the store were on sale.
    b. *Some* of the sweaters in the store were on sale.

2. Mrs. O'Grady used the milk, which had come from her cows, to make fresh ice cream.
    a. *All* of the milk came from Mrs. O'Grady's cows.
    b. *Some* of the milk came from Mrs. O'Grady's cows.

3. Kevin put away the towels, which had been laundered and folded.
    a. *All* of the towels had been laundered.
    b. *Some* of the towels had been laundered.

4. The women, whose husbands worked for ABC Company, formed a social group.

    a. *All* of their husbands worked for ABC Company.

    b. *Some* of their husbands worked for ABC Company.

5. The candidates who participated in last night's debate all expressed a concern for the homeless.

    a. *All* of the candidates participated in last night's debate.

    b. *Some* of the candidates participated in last night's debate.

6. I would like to speak to the mechanic, who worked on my car yesterday.

    a. The garage has *only one* mechanic.

    b. The garage has *more than one* mechanic.

■ **Quiz 5:** **Using expressions of quantity and possessive pronouns in adjective clauses.**

    A. Combine the sentences, using the second sentence as an adjective clause.

1. Rescuers had to navigate the flooded town in rowboats. Half of the town was under water.

    Rescuers had to navigate the flooded town, half of which was under water,

    in rowboats.

2. Mrs. White won first prize for her apple pie. The crust of the pie was exceptionally light and flaky.

    _____

    _____

3. When Craig got a new job in California, his wife had to find a new job and his children had to change schools. This was a very difficult situation for everyone.

    _____

    _____

4. The repairs to Jane's car were finished the same day. She was very pleased about that.

    _____

    _____

5. Mr. Carter talked to the large group of college students. Many of them did not know that he used to be the president.

_____

_____

6. The workers attended the meeting about the merger of the two companies. Most of their jobs were in danger because of consolidation and cost-cutting.

_____

_____

B. Decide if the adjective clause modifies a noun or the whole sentence. If the adjective clause modifies a noun, write *the noun.* If the adjective clause modifies a sentence, write *the sentence.*

1. Sally missed the bus, which made her late for work. _____*the sentence*_____

2. Sally missed the 28 Bus, which she usually takes to work. _____

3. The professor gave the students a long explanation about the homework assignment, which totally confused them. _____

4. The professor gave the students 20 pages of homework, which made all of the students groan. _____

5. Mrs. Anderson used to live in Dalian, which is a city in northeastern China.

_____

6. Max used to live in Dalian, which was one of the most interesting times in his life. _____

■ Quiz 6:   Reducing adjective clauses to adjective phrases.

Change the adjective clauses to adjective phrases, if possible.

1. Miriam attends Westlake Junior College, ~~which was~~ established by German immigrants in 1837.

2. The books that Alex needs for his research paper are available only at the main library.

3. The contestant who answers all ten questions correctly in less than one minute will win $64,000.

4. Pam is taking the train that is leaving for Budapest at 9:08 P.M.

5. This marble statue, which was sculpted by Bernini in 1678, is expected to sell for more than a million dollars at auction.

6. Mrs. North, whose son is enrolled at North Coast University, tells all her friends about her son's excellent academic record.

7. The new airport, which began construction two years ago, is expected to open by summer of next year.

8. My father is looking for a recliner that is covered in dark brown leather.

9. Firemen are quite concerned because the hills that surround the city are very dry and could easily catch fire.

10. You need to speak to the woman who is talking on the telephone.

11. Children who have dirty hands must wash them before they can eat dinner.

■ CHAPTER 13 TEST

A. After each paragraph is a short sentence. Add an adjective clause to the sentence to clarify its meaning.

1. Today is November 21st. John borrowed a book from the library a few weeks ago. It was due on November 20th. Mary borrowed a book from the library a few days ago. It is due on December 2nd.

   The book is overdue.

   _____*The book that John borrowed is overdue.*_____

2. John and Mary bought new shirts. John went to a party and spilled wine on his new shirt. Mary went to the same party, but she didn't spill anything on her shirt.

   The shirt has to be cleaned.

   _____

   _____

3. Mary has two neighbors. Both of them have dogs. One of the dogs is well behaved. It is very friendly and stays in its own yard. The other dog always gets out of its yard. When Mary came home today, she found dirt all over her driveway. A dog had dug a big hole in her flower bed.

   Mary needs to talk to the neighbor.

   _____

   _____

4. John takes the bus to and from work. In the morning, the buses are crowded. John rarely gets a seat. In the afternoon, there are far fewer people on the buses, and John often gets a seat.

   The bus is crowded.

   _____

   _____

5. John and Mary interviewed people for a job at their company. John interviewed a very capable woman. She had excellent communication skills and three years of experience. Mary interviewed another woman. She also had very good communication skills, but she had no experience in their company's area of business.

   John and Mary decided to hire the woman.

   _____

   _____

6. Mary has flower beds in front of and in back of her house. The flowers in the front yard get lots of sun and grow very well. The flowers in the back yard are not as successful. They are in the shade of the house, so they get less sun.

The flowers look wonderful.

_____

_____

7. John was in a long meeting. During the break, coffee and tea were served in the meeting room. John wanted to smoke a cigarette. The speaker announced that smokers had to go outside to the patio.

The people had to go outside.

_____

_____

8. John and Mary's boss is trying to arrange a meeting about the new project. He asks both John and Mary for their schedules for the next week. John is free on Monday, Tuesday, and Wednesday afternoon. Mary is free on Tuesday and Thursday afternoon.

Their boss is trying to find a time.

_____

_____

9. Mary has run out of milk, and some guests are arriving in 20 minutes. There is a large supermarket about half a mile away. Because people are going home from work, the parking lot at the supermarket will probably be crowded. There is also a little grocery store two blocks from Mary's house. She can walk there and back in 10 minutes.

Mary is going to go to the store.

_____

_____

10. Mary is getting ready for a job interview. She has two suits. One was a gift from her mother. It is dark blue and very conservative. Mary bought the other suit, which is forest green and looks well on Mary. Mary is very disappointed to find a food stain on the green skirt.

Mary is going to wear the suit to her interview.

_____

_____

11. Parking near John's house is always difficult. John's house is on Fremont Avenue, a busy street with lots of stores and banks. John can never find a parking space on that street. Behind John's house is Taylor Street. A lot of shoppers try to find parking on this street, but it is still less crowded than Fremont Avenue. John usually ends up parking here.

The street usually has some parking.

_____

_____

B. Combine the sentences, using the second sentence as an adjective clause or adjective phrase.

1. Brenda is going to return her new TV set to the store. The picture on her new TV set is fuzzy and flickers.

Brenda is going to return her new TV set, the picture on which is fuzzy and

flickers, to the store.

2. After working out in the weight room for 35 minutes, John took a quick shower and then soaked in the Jacuzzi. That felt very good.

_____

_____

3. Mr. Frank Brown is going to give a lecture at the Civic Auditorium. Mr. Brown is a well-known authority on World War I.

_____

_____

4. Tim is going to throw away his old suitcase. One of the wheels of the suitcase is broken.

_____

_____

5. The interview committee read the resumes of over 200 applicants. Only ten of them would be chosen for in-person interviews.

_____

_____

6. The temperature in the Northeast was above 100 degrees for a week. This caused the deaths of several elderly people and young children.

_____

_____

CHAPTER *14*
Gerunds and Infinitives, Part 1

■ **Quiz 1:** Using gerunds as the objects of prepositions.

Using the words in parentheses, complete the sentences with your own words.

1. Margaret forgave her sister *(break)* _____*for breaking her favorite vase.*_____

2. Mrs. Grant is devoted *(help)* _____

3. Larry is thinking *(go)* _____

4. My baby shows me she is hungry *(cry)* _____

5. Sarah is not used *(wear)* _____

6. Our class is responsible *(clean)* _____

7. Everyone is looking forward *(have)* _____

8. All of the students are worried *(pass)* _____

9. Fred fixed his broken eyeglasses *(use)* _____

10. Are you interested *(come)* _____

11. Do you really think that Sonya is guilty *(sell)* _____

■ **Quiz 2:** *Go* + gerund and special expressions followed by *-ing*.

Create sentences from the given verb combinations.

1. have difficulty + open

   _____ *I had difficulty opening that bottle.* _____

2. catch + listen

   _____

3. go + hike

   _____

4. spend + choose

   _____

5. sit + watch

   _____

6. go + shop

   _____

7. have a hard time + learn

   _____

8. waste + look

   _____

9. have fun + visit

   _____

10. stand + wait

    _____

11. find + dig

    _____

■ **Quiz 3:**   Common verbs followed by either infinitives or gerunds.

Complete each sentence with a gerund or an infinitive.

1. Mr. Lee asked his wife _____*to pass*_____ the butter.

2. Lucy enjoys _____ a few games of tennis on weekends.

3. Jenny hopes _____ her 40th birthday on a cruise ship to Hawaii.

4. Charles can't stand _____ in the park when it rains.

5. Olga needed _____ a plumber when her bathroom sink sprang a leak.

6. The fireman warned the bystanders _____ behind the barriers and away from the flames.

7. Ann refused _____ the party because she always ends up doing all the work.

8. Nancy forgot _____ the heat when she left the house, so the house was very warm when she returned home.

9. London expects _____ more than a million visitors for New Year's Eve.

10. Mrs. Allen suggested _____ flowers along the fence to cheer up the property.

11. The insurance agent encouraged Mrs. Davidson _____ her diamonds in a safe deposit box at the bank.

12. Kathy tried _____ her hair long, but long hair was too much trouble to take care of.

13. The Commonwealth Club invited the president of the United States _____ at their next meeting.

14. Paulo would like _____ to Brazil for the holidays, but he doesn't have enough time.

15. I remember _____ my grandmother's perfume whenever I visited her small apartment in San Francisco.

■ **Quiz 4:** *It* + infinitive; gerunds and infinitives as subjects.

A. Create sentences beginning with *it*. Use a form of the given expression in your sentence, followed by an infinitive phrase.

1. be enjoyable   *It is enjoyable to walk barefoot on the sand at the beach.*

2. take a long time   _____

3. should not be hard _____

4. might be boring   _____

5. cost a lot   _____

6. be unusual   _____

B. Rewrite the sentences you wrote for Part A. Use gerund phrases for your subjects.

1. _____*Walking barefoot on the sand at the beach is enjoyable.*_____

2. _____

3. _____

4. _____

5. _____

6. _____

■ CHAPTER 14 TEST

Complete the sentences, using a gerund or infinitive of an appropriate verb. Add an appropriate preposition if needed.

1. Paul Moore is guilty _____*of stealing*_____ $2 million from his former employer. He is being sentenced to five years in prison.

2. It has been raining for three days. John is really tired _____ indoors and not being able to go outside and play.

3. Cynthia apologized to her sister _____ her jewelry without asking permission. She promised that she would never do it again.

4. Kathy has spent a lot of time _____ this lesson. She hopes

   _____ a good grade on the next quiz.

5. Tim remembers _____ his briefcase home from work, but now he can't find it.

6. _____ an apple to the teacher is a traditional way for a student to thank a teacher in the United States.

7. Michael's car is making strange noises and needs _____ by a mechanic right away.

8. It is common for Jim _____ appointments because he is so busy.

9. Cindy doesn't enjoy _____ in line at the supermarket. That's

   why she tries _____ to the supermarket early in the afternoon or very late at night.

10. Mary's allergies were very bad last spring, and she couldn't help

    _____ all the time.

11. Philip is not very good _____, so he needs _____ someone to cater the food for his party.

12. Kevin is interested _____ Russian because he is going to

    Moscow next summer _____ his uncle.

13. Janice never goes _____ because she can't stand the cold weather.

14. When Tom decided _____ a new car for the family, his wife

suggested _____ on the Internet _____ some
research.

15. Before a patient starts _____ a new medicine, the correct dosage

needs _____ by the doctor.

16. Nancy was bored _____ TV, so she began _____
a book that she had borrowed from the library.

17. It was exhausting for Martha _____ all of the job applications,

but she is determined _____ a good supervisor for her
department.

18. Sam defrosted the frozen hamburger _____ it in the microwave
oven.

19. _____ two small children is a round-the-clock job. Barbara has

no time _____ .

20. Susan took a vacation to Hawaii. She spent six days _____ on a
white sand beach with a good book and a cold drink.

Name _____ Class _____ Date _____

CHAPTER 15
Gerunds and Infinitives, Part 2

■ Quiz 1:   Infinitive of purpose: *in order to.*

Read the story. Use information from the story to complete the sentences.

Some friends and I decided to take a vacation in Canada. We chose a cross-country trip by train, with a three-day stop in Banff. I really needed rest and relaxation because I had been working 60-hour weeks. We were going by train because my friend Josef is a train enthusiast. He told us that half of the trip would take place on an historic train with a steam engine from the 1910s. When he found out about the old train, nothing could stop Josef from going with us. Mariela was excited because of our stop in Banff. She had heard about the natural beauty of the mountains and lakes. She is a keen photographer, and she was looking forward to taking lots of pictures. Pauline was also looking forward to the trip, but she had a special reason to be excited. Her French boyfriend, Claude, would meet her in Toronto at the end of our trip. We all had different reasons for wanting to go on this vacation, but we all had one thing in common. We were good friends, and we wanted to spend some time together.

1. I was going on this trip _____*in order to get some much needed rest.*_____

2. Josef was going on this trip _____

   _____

3. Mariela was going on this trip _____

   _____

4. Pauline was going on this trip _____

   _____

5. Claude was flying to Toronto _____

   _____

■ **Quiz 2:** Adjectives followed by infinitives.

Answer the questions. Use infinitive phrases in your completions.

1. What is something that you are eager to do when you have enough money?

   I am eager to visit the pyramids in Egypt.

2. When is a person ready to get married?

   _____

3. What is likely to happen to a student who does not study or review?

   _____

4. What is something that you are willing to do that many people don't like to do?

   _____

5. What is something that you are certain to do next year?

   _____

6. What should one be prepared to do if one's house catches on fire?

   _____

7. What is one thing that you have been lucky to find?

   _____

8. What is one place that most people are reluctant to go?

   _____

9. What is one thing that you were surprised to discover about learning English?

   _____

10. What is one place that you are determined to see before you die?

    _____

11. What is something that you are always careful to do well?

    _____

■ **Quiz 3:** Using infinitives with *too* and *enough*

Complete the sentence using **too** or **enough** and the word in parentheses. Then write a second sentence with a similar meaning.

1. That rock is *(heavy)* _____*too heavy*_____ for me to lift.

   _____*I am not strong enough to lift it.*_____

2. I had better stay home. I am *(sick)* _____ to go to work.

   _____

3. My daughter is not *(tall)* _____ to ride on the roller coaster.

   _____

4. All the other cars are passing us. You are driving *(slow)* _____
   for the speed limit.

   _____

5. You need to put the soup back in the microwave for a few more minutes. It isn't

   (hot) _____ yet.

   _____

6. Here's another mistake. You are not checking your homework *(carefully)*

   _____ .

   _____

■ **Quiz 4:** Using gerunds or passive infinitives following *need.*

Supply an appropriate form of the verbs in parentheses.

1. My car is really dirty. I haven't washed it in three weeks. I need *(wash)*

   ___*to wash*___ my car, and it needs *(wash)* _____ soon!

2. My last composition had too many errors. The teacher told me that it needed

   (revise) _____. I need *(hand)* _____ it in by next Tuesday.

3. Nancy bought a large roast for dinner. It needs *(cook)* _____

   for at least three hours, so Nancy needs *(start)* _____ cooking by 2 o'clock.

4. These socks have holes in both toes and heels. They need *(throw)* _____ away.

5. You need *(fill out)* _____ Parts A and B on the form. Part C is

   optional and does not need *(fill out)* _____ today.

6. My brother is a fireman. He wasn't able to come with me because he needed

   (answer) _____ an emergency fire alarm.

7. The Gows are moving to their new house next month, so their current house needs

   (sell) _____ immediately.

■ **Quiz 5:** Using a possessive to modify a gerund.

Change the noun clauses into gerund phrases.

1. With this bad weather, we are worried that they will be late for their flight.
   ___*With this bad weather, we are worried about their being late for their flight.*___

2. You should take advantage of the fact that they are selling phone service for 50 percent off.

   _____

   _____

3. I'm sure that Mr. Grant will apologize for the fact that his children broke your kitchen window with a baseball.

   _____

   _____

4. Fatima's husband has been complaining that she goes shopping every weekend and spends a lot of money.

_____

_____

5. Although I love having houseguests, I am looking forward to the fact that they will leave soon.

_____

_____

6. The fact that Mr. Wah divorced his wife after 23 years stunned everyone.

_____

_____

7. Mark was very proud that his mother returned to school to finish her college education.

_____

_____

8. Martha is always afraid that her husband will not be dressed before their dinner guests arrive.

_____

_____

9. The manager resented the fact that his employee talked to the vice-president before he talked to him.

_____

_____

10. I can't stand the fact that they always complain but never do anything to help improve the situation.

_____

_____

11. Matthew is prepared for the fact that his opponent will try to steal the ball from him.

_____

_____

■ **Quiz 6:** Using verbs of perception.

Complete the sentences with any appropriate verbs.

1. The little boy noticed someone _____*hiding*_____ in the bushes in front of the house, so he ran inside to tell his father.

2. Polly smelled something _____ and realized that she had forgotten that rice was cooking on the stove.

3. Ivan watched the other boys _____ their kites and wished that his kite were still in one piece.

4. Jake was eating dinner at his friend's house when he felt something

   _____ against his leg. He looked down and saw his friend's cat.

5. Many people claim to have seen the plane _____ before it plunged into the sea.

6. When I take my little daughter to the doctor, I have to wait outside because I hate

   to hear her _____ when the doctor gives her a shot.

7. Carlos looked at the elephant _____ in the middle of the street. He couldn't believe his eyes!

8. When Helen's food is ready, she hears the microwave oven

   _____ .

9. At the Simon Pearce mill, Rosalyn was fascinated by the glassblower and watched

   him _____ a hot piece of glass into a lovely vase.

10. When you are waiting in the subway station, you always know a train is coming

    because you can feel the ground _____ .

11. Scientists have been able to observe stars _____ thanks to the power of the new telescopes.

■ **Quiz 7:** Using *let, help, make, have,* and *get.*

Complete the sentences with verb phrases.

1. My parents let me _____*stay up late on weekends.*_____

2. I'm not very strong. I always have my older brother _____

3. I don't understand this assignment. Can you help me _____

4. At the wedding, the bride even got my father _____

5. Because the jeans were too expensive, Carol's husband made her _____

_____

6. If you get lost, a policeman can help you _____

7. Do you think the teacher will let us _____

8. After three hours, Sheila finally got her computer _____

9. The coach had all of the players _____

10. The bad weather might make us _____

11. I'm tired of doing homework. Let's _____

■ CHAPTER 15 TEST

A. Use each set of words to write a sentence containing a gerund or an infinitive. All the sentences should follow one of these two themes: *school* or *a vacation*.

1. eager / take

    I'm eager to take an English class next semester.

2. shocked / get

    _____

3. determined / get

    _____

4. too tired / finish

    _____

5. enough time / go

    _____

6. need / plan

    _____

7. consider / buy

    _____

8. hear / talk

    _____

9. help / find

    _____

10. have / call

    _____

11. stop / read

    _____

B. Correct the errors.

going   *to get / for*
1. Tom is thinking about ~~to go~~ to graduate school ~~for getting~~ a Master's degree.

2. Our house needs to repair and paint before we can consider to sell it.

3. There isn't enough time to us for finishing all of the reports by Friday.

4. Sally was sorry to have being late and she apologized to have missed part of the presentation.

5. Jason has been thinking about he moving out of the house and find a job.

6. I heard the rain fell on the roof and realized that I needed bringing an umbrella with me.

7. My doctor made me to wait 45 minutes before he would see me.

8. Mrs. Won wouldn't let her son played football because she was worried about he gets hurt.

9. These jeans are tight enough for me to wear anymore.

10. The president had the company putting off send out its annual report.

11. We all look forward to you will give the valedictory speech at the graduation.

CHAPTER 16
Coordinating Conjunctions

■ **Quiz 1:** **Parallel structure.**

Combine the sentences into one concise sentence that contains parallel structure. Punctuate carefully.

1. The food was tasty.
   The food was cheap.
   The food was plentiful.

   _____*The food was tasty, cheap, and plentiful.*_____

2. The new magazine was colorful.
   The new magazine was glossy.
   The new magazine had lots of photographs.
   The new magazine had lots of advertising.

   _____

3. The fireman put out a fire.
   The fireman rescued a cat stuck in a tree.
   The fireman helped a man who had had a heart attack.

   _____

4. In Brazil, I saw white sand beaches.
   In Brazil, I saw beautiful young women.
   In Brazil, I saw beautiful young men.
   In Brazil, I saw crystal clear blue water.

   _____

5. When Jane got home from work, she took off her suit.
   She took off her high-heeled shoes.
   She put on an old pair of jeans.
   She put on an old pair of slippers.
   She put on a warm wool sweater.

   _____

6. For dinner, Kevin ate slices of roast beef with gravy.
   For dinner, Kevin ate rice with gravy.
   For dinner, Kevin ate string beans.
   For dinner, Kevin drank a glass of wine.

   _____

■ **Quiz 2:** **Paired conjunctions.**

Use paired conjunctions to combine the sentences or clauses.

1. Philip doesn't like to wake up early in the morning. Francis doesn't like to wake up early in the morning.

    _____*Neither Philip nor Francis likes to wake up early in the morning.*_____

2. Cindy will babysit the kids this evening, or Mrs. Smith will babysit the kids this evening.

    _____

3. During the holiday weekend, the parking lots at San Francisco International Airport were full. During the holiday weekend, the parking lots at San Jose Airport were full.

    _____

4. Bread should be stored in the freezer instead of the refrigerator. Flour should be stored in the freezer instead of the refrigerator.

    _____

5. Arthur has never been to Disneyland. His cousins have never been to Disneyland.

    _____

6. The earthquake knocked over several freeways. The earthquake broke gas and water lines.

    _____

7. Philip doesn't want to go to college. Philip doesn't want to find a job.

    _____

8. The contractor will try to repair the broken fence, or she will tear down the fence and replace it.

    _____

9. Oranges are a good source of vitamin C. Cabbage is a good source of vitamin C.

    _____

10. Mayoral candidate Jim Brown did not talk about the homeless problem. Mayoral candidate Alicia Taylor did not talk about the homeless problem.

    _____

11. The severe rainstorm flooded basements and sewers. The severe rainstorm caused mudslides.

    _____

■ **Quiz 3:** Combining independent clauses with coordinating conjunctions.

Punctuate the sentences by adding commas or periods. Do not add any words. Capitalize where necessary.

1. The gardener pruned the rose bushes and clipped the hedges. *H*e swept up the dead leaves, and he added fertilizer to the vegetable beds.

2. Polly was looking for a new camera for her brother's birthday she wanted a large selection and good prices so she used the Internet to do her shopping.

3. Both Silvia and her husband love the rock band The Rolling Stones but they refuse to pay $80 a ticket to attend a concert.

4. Myron has written short stories and poems for the school literary magazine and sports and feature articles for the school newspaper.

5. Acme Toy Company continues to produce dolls metal cars construction sets and action figures but it no longer makes bicycles or board games.

6. Flights 2058 and 2065 to Los Angeles have been delayed but Flight 2061 is departing on time I can get you a seat on Flight 2061.

7. I have tried the pineapple diet I have tried the starch diet and the protein diet too but none of them worked.

8. The weather forecaster predicts heavy fog and light drizzle for the morning but clear skies and sunshine for the late afternoon.

9. Mary doesn't like to drink tea or decaffeinated coffee so we need to pick up some regular coffee for her.

10. Bicycles motorcycles and handicapped drivers' cars can be parked in Lot A but everyone else needs to park in Lots B or C.

11. Barbara has had many different jobs she has been a flight attendant a sales clerk a waitress and a receptionist but now she has her MBA and is the regional manager for a large multinational corporation.

■ CHAPTER 16 TEST

Combine the sentences, using conjunctions and parallel structure. Punctuate carefully.

1. John couldn't find a good gift for his mother. John couldn't find a good gift for his aunt. He finally bought them gift certificates instead.

   _____ John could find a good gift neither for his mother nor for his aunt, so he finally_____

   _____ bought them gift certificates instead._____

2. Linda has traveled by car. Linda has traveled by bus. Linda has traveled by train. Linda has not traveled by ship. Linda has not traveled by plane. Linda has not traveled by balloon.

   _____

   _____

   _____

3. Thomas has read about computers. Thomas has read about the Internet. Thomas has taken classes in computer programming. Thomas has taken classes in computer applications.

   _____

   _____

   _____

4. At her surprise birthday party, Gloria was surprised to see her high school friends. Gloria was surprised to see her aunt and uncle from New York City. Gloria was surprised to see her old college roommate. She was disappointed not to see her sister. She was disappointed not to see her niece.

   _____

   _____

   _____

5. Last winter, Cincinnati experienced terrible storms. Cincinnati experienced terrible flooding. Cincinnati experienced unending rains. Cincinnati experienced devastating tornadoes. Cincinnati experienced devastating hail.

   _____

   _____

   _____

6. Next weekend, Shirley may visit her grandmother.   She may visit her sister.   She may do some shopping.   She may take in a movie.   She has to do the laundry.   She has to clean the bathroom.

   _____

   _____

   _____

7. Anita loves to play volleyball.   Sandra loves to play volleyball.   Betty doesn't like sports.   Jackie doesn't like sports.

   _____

   _____

   _____

8. Last night, Larry watched some TV.   Larry surfed on the Internet.   Larry listened to some music.   Larry read the newspaper.   Today, Larry has to do some serious work.

   _____

   _____

   _____

9. Mr. Kincaid owns real estate.   Mr. Kincaid owns stocks.   Mr. Kincaid owns bonds.   Mr. Kincaid has to sell some stocks to pay his taxes.   Mr. Kincaid has to sell some bonds to pay his taxes.

   _____

   _____

   _____

10. Craig has good computer skills and can type 70 words a minute.   Jean has good computer skills and can type 70 words a minute.   They both got jobs as executive secretaries.

   _____

   _____

   _____

11. French is an Indo-European language.   German is an Indo-European language.   Chinese is not an Indo-European language.   Korean is not an Indo-European language.

   _____

   _____

   _____

12. It was an extremely cold day. Mark put on a heavy sweater. Mark put on a warm jacket. Mark didn't wear a hat. Mark didn't wear a scarf.

_____

_____

_____

13. This apartment has no air conditioning. This apartment has no closet space. This apartment has a broken stove. This apartment has peeling paint. I really need to find a new apartment.

_____

_____

_____

14. When Steve had his skiing accident, he broke two ribs. He broke his collarbone. He broke his wrist. He broke his arm. He didn't sustain any head injury. He didn't sustain any spinal injury.

_____

_____

_____

15. I can sleep on the couch. I can sleep on the floor. You don't have to be so polite. You don't have to give me your bed.

_____

_____

_____

16. This magazine has interesting articles about Hawaii. This magazine has interesting articles about mountain climbing. This magazine has interesting articles about different cultural customs. This magazine has useful articles about getting the best airfares. This magazine has useful articles about the best times of year to travel.

_____

_____

_____

CHAPTER 17
Adverb Clauses

■ **Quiz 1:** Using adverb clauses to show cause and effect.

Combine the sentences, using the word or phrase in parentheses. Add commas where necessary.

1. Ellen took a nap when she got home from work. Ellen had had a very difficult day at her job. *(because)*

   Ellen took a nap when she got home from work because she had had a very

   difficult day at her job.

2. John arrived at the airport just 10 minutes before his flight was scheduled to depart. John nearly missed his plane. *(because)*

   _____

   _____

3. The rain has stopped. We can open the windows and get some fresh air. *(now that)*

   _____

   _____

4. We will have to contact Mr. Adams by mail. Mr. Adams has neither e-mail nor a fax machine. *(since)*

   _____

   _____

5. Sue did not enjoy going to the movies. Sue had left her eyeglasses at home. *(because)*

   _____

   _____

6. Larry has to do a lot of traveling. Larry is the senior manager for the western division of his company. *(now that)*

_____

_____

7. We can stay up late and talk. We don't have to go to work tomorrow. *(since)*

_____

_____

8. I need to find a new place to get my hair cut. My barber has retired after 25 years. *(now that)*

_____

_____

9. The two groups refused to sign the peace treaty. Fighting between the two groups has begun again. *(because)*

_____

_____

10. Future funding for the space program is uncertain. The last three space missions failed. *(since)*

_____

_____

11. The price of cigarettes has risen 400 percent in the last three years. Cigarette taxes have risen. *(because)*

_____

_____

■ **Quiz 2:** Using adverb clauses to express cause and effect, unexpected result, and direct contrast.

Choose the clause that best completes each sentence.

1. __*b*__ The flight has been delayed because

2. _____ The flight has been delayed even though

3. _____ John's flight has been delayed for three hours, while

4. _____ I finished reading the book although

5. _____ I usually read a book because

6. _____ I think this book is quite interesting, while

7. _____ The weather this month has been terrible, whereas

8. _____ The weather this month has been terrible because

9. _____ Even though the weather this month has been terrible,

10. _____ Because the tuition is very low,

11. _____ Even though the tuition is very low,

a. the quality of the class offerings is good.

b. there is heavy fog at the San Francisco airport.

c. a wet weather system has moved down from Alaska.

d. I have been busy with plenty of jobs indoors.

e. there doesn't seem to be any problem with the weather.

f. Mary's flight is going to leave on time.

g. last month we had sunny days almost every day.

h. my brother refused to read it.

i. it received a good review in the newspaper.

j. I also think that it was poorly written.

k. more people can take advantage of the class offerings.

■ **Quiz 3:** **Expressing conditions in adverb clauses: *if*-clauses.**

Make two sentences from the given possibilities. Use *if*.

1. It might rain tomorrow.

   If it rains tomorrow, I will bring an umbrella.

   If it rains tomorrow, I won't have to water my garden.

2. You might forget to set your alarm clock.

   _____

   _____

3. The price of gasoline may go up.

   _____

   _____

4. Your boss might not give you a raise.

   _____

   _____

5. The police might stop Larry for driving above the speed limit.

   _____

   _____

6. You might need to talk with me tomorrow.

   _____

   _____

■ **Quiz 4:** Adverb clauses of condition: *whether or not, even if, in case,* and *in the event that.*

Complete the sentences. Add commas if necessary.

1. Whether or not I feel well ____*, I will attend the meeting tomorrow night.* _____

2. Susan will leave work today at 4:00 P.M. even if _____

3. In case you need to contact us _____

4. In the event that an earthquake occurs _____

5. We will have a picnic in the park whether or not _____

6. Even if John gets a low score on the next quiz _____

■ **Quiz 5:** Using adverb clauses to express condition: using *unless* and *only if.*

Complete the sentences, using **unless** or **only if**.

1. _____*Unless*_____ the meeting goes late, I will meet you at the restaurant at 6:30 P.M.

2. I will be late for dinner _____ the meeting goes late.

3. _____ I have problems with my homework will I call you.

4. The project will be completed on time _____ there is a problem with the new design.

5. _____ your shoes are clean can you come into the house.

6. _____ the store does not accept credit cards will I need to borrow some money from you.

7. I like almost all ice cream. I dislike ice cream _____ it contains walnuts.

8. I will have to retype the entire report _____ I can't find the original file on my computer.

9. _____ your library books are returned on time, you will need to pay a fine.

10. I forgot my key, but my sister can let us into the house _____ she is out with her friends.

11. I will let you borrow my car _____ you promise that you will be extra careful.

■ CHAPTER 17 TEST

A. Complete the sentences. Punctuate carefully.

1. Now that my son has his driver's license

    _____, he can drive to the mall by himself._

2. Unless the weather improves by tomorrow

    _____

3. Even if you aren't sure about the correct answer

    _____

4. Lisa can't drive us to the airport because

    _____

5. If the doctor discovers that the cancer has returned

    _____

6. You have to stay until the end of the meeting whether or not

    _____

7. According to a public opinion poll, some people enjoy receiving junk mail whereas

    _____

8. In the event that you have a car accident

    _____

9. My father will loan me the money for a new car only if

    _____

10. My orange tree failed to produce any oranges this year because

    _____

11. Only if it is an emergency

    _____

B. Complete the sentences by using *because*, *even though*, *if*, or *unless*.

1. Susan takes very good care of her emerald ring _____*because*_____ it has been passed down from mother to daughter for five generations.

2. _____ the local government builds a dam here, hundreds of acres of farmland will be under water.

3. _____ Joe turned on the air conditioner an hour ago, the room is still hot and stuffy.

4. _____ you wait for the soup to cool a little bit, you will burn your mouth.

5. Tim will not be able to play basketball anymore _____ he damages his knee again.

6. Mary prefers to communicate by e-mail _____ it is fast and convenient.

7. _____ Max has lost a lot of weight, his health has not improved

_____ he still refuses to do any exercise.

8. The workers refused to work on New Year's Eve _____ the company promised to pay them double their usual wage.

9. _____ Sam improves his grades in chemistry and biology, he will never be able to get into medical school.

10. _____ the test was very easy, Patricia worked on it for more than an hour to make sure that she didn't make any mistakes.

11. _____ Peter Smith wins the election for president, he promises to lower taxes and restore people's faith in government.

12. Maria has decided to marry Harry _____ she doesn't love him

_____ he has a lot of money and will be a good provider for her children.

13. You can't drive a car by yourself _____ you have only a learner's permit. You'll have to wait until you have a real driver's license.

14. _____ the technician can diagnose the problem with Jimmy's computer, Jimmy may have to buy a new one.

CHAPTER 18
Reduction of Adverb Clauses to Modifying Adverbial Phrases

■ **Quiz 1:**   Changing time clauses to modifying adverbial phrases.

Change the adverb clauses to modifying adverbial phrases if possible. If not possible, write **No change**.

1. While John was cleaning out his garage, he found his old high school yearbooks.

    While cleaning out his garage, John found his old high school yearbooks.

2. After John cleaned out the garage, Mary reorganized the shelves and cabinets.

    _____

    _____

3. Before Mary threw anything away, she consulted with John to make sure it was okay.

    _____

    _____

4. Since they moved into their house in 1992, Mary and John have acquired a lot of furniture.

    _____

    _____

5. While the Wilsons were on vacation in Venice, Italy, they bought a lot of glass sculpture.

    _____

    _____

6. Before the Wilsons left Italy, they had all the sculpture sent to their home in the United States.

    _____

    _____

7. After the sculptures arrived, the Wilsons had to go to the Customs Office to pick them up.

_____

_____

8. Since they took their trip to Italy, the Wilsons have been collecting glass from all over the world.

_____

_____

9. Before Joe bought a new car, his sister helped him do some research on the Internet.

_____

_____

10. While Joe's sister was searching for information, she found two other cars that she thought would interest him.

_____

_____

11. After Joe read all the articles that his sister had found for him, Joe chose which car he wanted.

_____

_____

■ **Quiz 2:** **Expressing cause and effect in modifying adverbial phrases.**

A. Change the adverb clauses to modifying adverbial phrases.

1. While Tim was taking a shower, he was shocked when the hot water suddenly ran cold.

    (While) Taking a shower, Tim was shocked when the hot water suddenly

    ran cold.

2. While Pete was delivering newspapers on his bicycle, he was attacked by a large, ferocious dog.

    _____

    _____

3. Because Sally was not able to manage her time well, she was late with all of her class assignments.

   _____

   _____

4. Because Mike has been working 14 hours a day at two different jobs, he does little more than sleep when he gets home.

   _____

   _____

5. While Jack was studying for his grammar test in the library, he fell asleep.

   _____

   _____

6. Because Clare doesn't have enough time to clean her house, she has a housecleaner who comes every other week.

   _____

   _____

B. Read each sentence. What is the meaning of the adverbial phrase? Write **because** or **while** to show the meaning.

1. Having received Alan's marriage proposal, Sue told all her friends that she was getting married. _____*because*_____

2. Standing in a long line at the post office, Betty read a book to pass the time.

   _____

3. Working on his quiz, Ken found that his pen had run out of ink. He had to borrow one from a classmate. _____

4. Being over 6 feet tall, Simon is always asked to try out for the basketball team.

   _____

5. Knowing the basics of plumbing and electrical wiring, Carla saves a lot of money by doing her own home repairs. _____

6. Flying in economy, Paul finds it difficult to get comfortable because of his long legs.

   _____

■ **Quiz 3:**   Using *upon* + *-ing* in modifying adverbial phrases.

Combine these sentences, using **upon** + **-ing**.

1. *first:* John received the good news about his new job.
   then: John immediately called his family.

   _____*Upon receiving the good news about his new job, John immediately*_____

   _____*called his family.*_____

2. *first:* Jane Peters was elected mayor of the city.
   then: She set up a committee to study the public schools.

   _____

   _____

3. *first:* Mrs. Alexander returned from a trip to Mexico.
   then: She started a small business that sold Mexican handicrafts.

   _____

   _____

4. *first:* Tina had her sixth baby.
   then: She said, "I think this will be my last one."

   _____

   _____

5. *first:* Minal finished her final exam.
   then: She breathed a sigh of relief.

   _____

   _____

6. *first:* Tom found a gold coin in the sand at the beach.
   then: He couldn't believe his good luck.

   _____

   _____

■ CHAPTER 18 TEST

A. Change the adverbial phrases into adverb clauses.

1. Upon being accepted to law school, John went out to celebrate.

    When John was accepted to law school, he went out to celebrate.

2. Lying in bed and feeling depressed, Joe wondered what he would do now that he no longer had a job.

    _____

3. Not having any money to buy a present for his mother, Johnny made her a birthday card.

    _____

4. After testing the drug on mice, the research scientists will test the drug on monkeys.

    _____

5. Since taking a course in public speaking, Alex has developed more self-confidence.

    _____

6. On arriving in London, the first thing Jane will do is have tea at the Ritz Hotel.

    _____

7. Confused about the directions to the party, Carol had to stop at a gas station to ask for help.

    _____

8. Before leaving for India, Brian had to get several shots to protect him from tropical diseases.

    _____

9. While talking with his accountant, Omar realized that starting his own business would be quite complicated.

    _____

10. Upon tasting Mrs. Wilson's blueberry pie, Chef Louis declared that it was the most delicious pie he had ever eaten.

    _____

11. Working in her garden, Susan disturbed a wasp's nest and was stung several times.

    _____

B. Combine the two sentences, using an adverb clause or modifying adverbial phrase.

1. I didn't want to interrupt your meeting. I left a message with your secretary.

   Not wanting to interrupt your meeting, I left a message with your secretary.

2. First the doctor explained the medical procedure. Then the doctor asked the patient if he had any questions.

   _____

3. George was standing on a ladder to change a light bulb. Suddenly, his dog ran by and knocked the ladder over.

   _____

4. Sam read a book about sharks. Sam has been afraid to swim in the ocean.

   _____

5. It began to rain. Luisa opened her umbrella.

   _____

6. My brother was playing basketball with his friends. He fell and sprained his ankle.

   _____

7. First Paul finished his homework assignment. Then he was free to watch TV for the rest of the evening.

   _____

8. Mr. Santos became a citizen. Afterward, the first thing he did was register to vote.

   _____

9. Mrs. Nguyen had no husband and three children. She had to work ten hours a day to keep them fed and clothed.

   _____

10. Jane didn't receive a package from her brother. She contacted the post office about tracking the package.

    _____

11. George graduated from the university with a degree in French history. He has been looking for a position at a university.

    _____

CHAPTER 19
Connectives That Express Cause and Effect, Contrast, and Condition

■ **Quiz 1:** Using *because, because of,* and *due to.*

Combine the sentences. Use the word in parentheses.

1. The Wilsons had to postpone the picnic. The weather was bad.

   a. *(because)* _____ *The Wilsons had to postpone the picnic because the weather was bad.*

   b. *(because of)* _____ *The Wilsons had to postpone the picnic because of bad weather.*

2. Mary had to retake the Introduction to Physics class. She got a failing grade.

   a. *(because)* _____

   _____

   b. *(because of)* _____

   _____

3. The minister of finance raised the interest rates. He was afraid of inflation.

   a. *(because)* _____

   _____

   b. *(because of)* _____

   _____

4. Although Bill wanted to study art, he majored in engineering. His father pressured him to do so.

   a. *(because)* _____

   _____

   b. *(because of)* _____

   _____

5. During the hot summer, ants come inside homes. They are searching for water.

a. *(because)* _____

_____

b. *(because of)* _____

_____

6. The space ship to Mars got lost. Scientists had made errors in their calculations.

a. *(because)* _____

_____

b. *(due to)* _____

_____

■ **Quiz 2:** **Summary of cause-and-effect patterns, including *therefore* and *consequently*.**
Rewrite the sentences, using the words in parentheses. Use appropriate punctuation.

1. The traffic on Highway 101 was jammed, so we took Highway 280 instead.
   (therefore)

   The traffic on Highway 101 was jammed. Therefore, we took

   Highway 280 instead.

2. Because of the crowds at the mall, Sally did her shopping over the Internet. *(so)*

   _____

   _____

3. Ron was late to work for the third time. Consequently, he was fired from his job.
   (because)

   _____

   _____

4. Because the stock market has risen 40 percent over the last year, fewer people are saving money in banks. *(because of)*

   _____

   _____

5. Many students come to the United States because it is easier to get admitted to a college. *(so)*

_____

_____

6. The movie is no longer showing in the theater, so we will have to wait until it comes out on video. *(therefore)*

_____

_____

7. Bill can't lift heavy objects due to the injury to his lower back. *(because)*

_____

_____

8. Larry heard that his friend was in the hospital. Therefore, he sent him a card and some flowers. *(consequently)*

_____

_____

9. The sweater Jane bought has a snag, so she needs to return it to the store and exchange it. *(due to)*

_____

_____

10. There have been many construction delays, so the extension to the subway line will not open on time. *(because)*

_____

_____

11. The house is now quite dilapidated because the previous owners never took care of it. *(so)*

_____

_____

■ **Quiz 3:**   Other ways of expressing cause and effect: *such . . . that, so . . . that,* and *so that.*

Complete the sentences with your own words.

1. Mary was so late that _____ *she missed the first half hour of the movie.* _____

2. The economy is doing so well that _____

3. John is such a liar that _____

4. Many African elephants are killed so that _____

5. Pat is such a good student that _____

6. Jim always checks his dictionary so that _____

7. Many people in the world are so poor that _____

8. Dr. Robinson's daughter's wedding was so expensive that _____

9. Tommy has such poor computer skills that _____

10. Robert bought a new computer so that _____

11. This is such a good book that _____

■ **Quiz 4:**   Showing contrast (unexpected result).

Complete the sentences with **but, despite, even though, nevertheless, so, because of, because,** or **therefore.** Add appropriate punctuation.

1. Ms. Gow had to lie down _____ *because of* _____ her splitting headache.

2. Roberto had his car repaired last week. _____ it is still not running smoothly.

3. _____ Thomas left his reading glasses at home he wasn't able to read the menu.

4. Howard is a careful driver _____ he never gets a traffic ticket.

5. _____ Emily skipped breakfast she still has a lot of energy.

6. Fewer people in the Bay Area can afford to buy a house _____ the sharp increase in home prices in the last six months.

7. Mr. Kwan is a rich man _____ he still refuses to buy his daughter a new car.

8. _____ his busy schedule, Ali still found time to coach his son's baseball team.

9. Mark collects old fountain pens, _____ he loves to visit antique stores wherever he goes.

10. _____ Martina fell in the ice skating competition, the judges still gave her high scores.

11. Omar was sending the package overseas _____ the postage was quite high.

12. Tarek is very afraid of dogs _____ he was bitten by one as a child.

13. _____ the favorable exchange rate, many people are going to Canada for vacations.

14. _____ the freeway has been widened to five lanes, the traffic is still terrible.

15. Anne really loves to eat mangoes, _____ she refuses to pay $2.00 for one.

16. Brian's office is going to get a new copier _____ the fact that the old one works fine.

■ **Quiz 5: Showing direct contrast.**

Write sentences contrasting two people that you know very well. Use the word or phrase in parentheses.

1. *(while)* _____ *Uncle Philip is very talkative, while Aunt Margaret is usually very quiet.*

2. *(but)* _____

3. *(however)* _____

4. *(whereas)* _____

5. *(on the other hand)* _____

6. *(while)* _____

■ **Quiz 6:** **Expressing conditions:** *otherwise* **and** *or else.*

Complete the sentences, punctuating carefully. Use capital letters where appropriate.

1. The weather had better . . . otherwise . . . .

    The weather had better improve. Otherwise, we will have to postpone our

    picnic.

2. I have to . . . or else . . . .

    _____

    _____

3. The government should . . . otherwise . . . .

    _____

    _____

4. People must . . . or else . . . .

    _____

    _____

5. Access to the Internet must be . . . otherwise . . . .

    _____

    _____

6. You should . . . or else . . . .

    _____

    _____

■ CHAPTER 19 TEST

A. Using the ideas of *to be warm* (or *to be cold*) and *to wear* (or *not to wear*), complete the sentences. Punctuate and capitalize correctly.

1. Even though it was a warm day _____*, I didn't wear a jacket.* _____

2. I didn't wear a jacket because _____

3. I need to wear a jacket otherwise _____

4. It was cold outside but _____

5. It was a warm day so _____

6. I didn't wear a jacket despite _____

7. It was a cold day consequently _____

8. Due to the cold weather _____

9. It was such a cold day that _____

10. I had better wear a jacket or else _____

11. It was a cold day however _____

12. Unless I wear a jacket _____

13. If it isn't warm outside _____

14. It is a warm day nevertheless _____

15. It was quite warm yesterday whereas _____

B. Complete the sentences in your own words, adding punctuation and capitalization.

1. As a child, I had very few toys on the other hand . . . .

   _____*As a child, I had very few toys. On the other hand, kids today have too*_____

   _____*many toys.*_____

2. The food at the Thai restaurant was so spicy that . . . .

   _____

   _____

3. Although Emily fertilized and watered her apple tree . . . .

_____

_____

4. Because of improvements in health care and medical treatment . . . .

_____

_____

5. Many people do not like cellular phones because . . . .

_____

_____

6. The government is going to reduce taxes so that . . . .

_____

_____

7. Unless Maria learns to drive a car . . . .

_____

_____

8. The recent freeze destroyed 80 percent of the orange crop therefore . . . .

_____

_____

9. Despite Martha's terrible experience in Hawaii last year . . . .

_____

_____

10. My Uncle James must lose weight and give up smoking or else . . . .

_____

_____

11. Karen refused to marry Tom even though . . . .

_____

_____

CHAPTER 20
Conditional Sentences and Wishes

■ **Quiz 1:** **True in the present or future.**

Write a sentence using *if* to show present or future possibility.

1. John might win the lottery.

_____*If John wins the lottery, he will buy a new car.*_____

2. Mary might go to Paris for vacation.

_____

_____

3. Geoffrey might lose his job.

_____

_____

4. Larry might not have enough money for a new car.

_____

_____

5. The price of gasoline might go up.

_____

_____

6. There might not be enough time to finish Chapter 20.

_____

_____

■ **Quiz 2:** Untrue (contrary to fact) in the present or future.

Write a sentence about yourself for each of these untrue conditions.

1. You are ten years younger.

   _____ *If I were ten years younger, I would major in computer science.* _____

2. You are ten years older.

   _____

3. You can speak and write English fluently.

   _____

4. You can predict the future.

   _____

5. You can fly.

   _____

6. You are a famous movie star.

   _____

■ **Quiz 3:** Untrue (contrary to fact) in the past.

Write an *if* sentence based on the information.

1. The weather was terrible yesterday. We wanted to go for a hike, but we didn't.

   _____ *We would have gone for a hike if the weather had not been terrible.* _____

2. Karen didn't invest any money in the stock market last year. She didn't make a lot of money.

   _____

3. Paula twisted her ankle. She couldn't finish the marathon. She was very disappointed.

   _____

4. Michael got three traffic tickets last year. His insurance rates went up.

_____

5. John interviewed for a job with Acme Corporation. They wanted him to move to their South Dakota office. He didn't want to move, so he didn't accept the job offer.

_____

6. Even though it wasn't warm, George wouldn't wear a jacket or sweater. He caught a very bad cold.

_____

7. Mr. Martinez tried to move the heavy sofa by himself. He pulled a muscle in his lower back.

_____

8. Linda's grandchildren came to visit her in the summer. Otherwise, she planned to visit them.

_____

9. Sally Smith was running for mayor. She lost the election by 253 votes.

_____

10. Alex bought some ice cream. He put it in the refrigerator by accident. It melted.

_____

11. Susie didn't practice the piano all week. She couldn't play her pieces for her lesson.

_____

■ **Quiz 4:**   Using progressive verb forms and "mixed time" in conditional sentences.

Complete the story, using the verbs in parentheses.

Paul is paying his monthly bills. He is very worried because there are a lot of bills. If he _____*hadn't spent*_____ (spend, not) so much money, he _____*wouldn't be*_____ (be, not) so worried now. What if he doesn't have enough money?

He looks at the bills one by one. The first one is for car repairs. If he _____ (send, not) his car to the garage for repairs, he _____ (save) $600. However, if he _____ (have, not) a car to drive for the last month, he _____ (be able to, not) go to work and he _____ (be able to, not) pay any bills now.

The second bill is for the rent. If he doesn't pay his rent, he _____ (have) no place to live, so he has to pay this bill. The next bill is for his dentist. Paul developed a serious toothache three weeks ago. If he _____ (go, not) to the dentist right away, his tooth _____ (give) him problems tomorrow.

The fourth bill is for repairs to his television. When Paul bought his television, he decided not to get an extended warranty. If he _____ (get) the warranty then, it _____ (cost) only $79 extra. Instead, he has to pay $150 for the repairs because the warranty has expired.

The fifth bill is for the department store. Paul bought four new shirts and three pairs of pants. The bill is for $450. If he _____ (buy) only one shirt and one pair of pants, he _____ (owe) only $125.

Paul can't believe how much money he spent over the past month. If he _____ (keep) track of his spending, he probably _____ (be, not) in this situation. After he pays his bills, if he _____ (have, not) enough money to live on, he will have to take money out of savings.

■ **Quiz 5:** Omitting *if* and implied conditions.

    A. Create sentences with the same meaning by omitting *if*.

    1. If we had a quorum, we could start the meeting.

       Had we a quorum, we could start the meeting.

    2. The disaster could have been avoided if the authorities had been more vigilant.

    3. If there should be more problems with your furnace, call this phone number.

    4. If the residents had received the warning earlier, fewer people would have been killed in the tornado.

    5. I would try to enjoy my youth more if I were sixteen again.

    6. If you should have any problems with your purchase, you can bring it back for a complete refund.

    B. Complete the sentences with your own words.

    1. I . . . , but I don't have enough time.

       I would come and visit, but I don't have enough time.

    2. I . . . , but I didn't have a car.

    3. Mary . . . , but she didn't have enough time to study.

    4. Mary . . . , but she has to pick her kids up from school.

5. The government . . . , but it doesn't have enough money.

_____

6. The government . . . , but it doesn't know how to.

_____

■ **Quiz 6:** Using *as if* or *as though*.

Complete each sentence with **as if** or **as though** and your own words.

1. I am so hungry. I feel . . . .

_____ *I feel as if I could eat a whole pizza all by myself.* _____

2. I am so tired. I feel . . . .

_____

3. Your room is such a mess. It looks . . . ,

_____

4. Are you feeling okay? You sound . . . .

_____

5. The show is about to start, and Linda still isn't here. It looks . . . .

_____

6. We really need to clean out the refrigerator. It smells . . . .

_____

■ **Quiz 7:** Verb forms following *wish*.

Complete the sentences with an appropriate verb form.

1. The mayor can't solve the homeless problem, but I wish she ____*could*____.

2. I don't live in California any more, but I wish I _____.

3. I have a terrible headache right now, but I wish I _____.

4. This blouse isn't on sale, but I wish it _____.

5. Aunt Rose couldn't come to my anniversary party, but I wish she

   _____.

6. The drugstore doesn't carry my favorite brand of shampoo anymore, but I wish it

   _____.

7. I'm not going to get an "A" in this class, but I wish I _____.

8. I got another parking ticket yesterday, but I wish I _____.

9. Elena didn't go to the concert last weekend, but she wishes she _____.

10. Mrs. Takasawa doesn't speak Japanese, but she wishes she _____.

11. My toddler can open the drawers in the kitchen, but I wish he _____.

12. Khalid's hair is turning gray, but he wishes it _____.

13. Brian isn't tall enough to ride on the roller coaster, but he wishes he

    _____.

14. I can't cook well, but I wish I _____.

15. My son is going to join the army, but I wish he _____.

16. Bill has gained a lot of weight, but he wishes he _____.

■ CHAPTER 20 TEST

A. Read the story.

Mary is sitting in the airport. She missed her flight, and she is feeling very angry and frustrated. The next flight will not leave for two hours.

Mary planned her trip very carefully. She called the taxi company the day before and made a reservation for 10 A.M. She had her suitcase packed and ready by 9:30 A.M. She was sure the taxi was going to come, so she didn't call to confirm her reservation. When the taxi had not arrived by 10:20, Mary called the taxi company. They had no record of her reservation. They sent out a taxi right away. Mary was so nervous about missing her flight that she left her purse on the table by the front door. Fortunately, she had her house keys in the suitcase pocket, but the taxi had to turn around and go back to Mary's house so that she could get her purse. Finally, the taxi was on the freeway to the airport. However, a terrible accident had occurred only ten minutes before, and the traffic was stuck. It took more than 45 minutes to get to the airport. By the time Mary ran up to the ticket counter, there was only five minutes before her flight was scheduled to leave. The clerk apologized and told her that it was too late to board her flight and that she would have to take the next one.

Write five *if* sentences based on the events in the story.

Example: _____ *If Mary had not missed her flight, she would not be feeling angry*

_____ *and frustrated.*

1. _____

_____

2. _____

_____

3. _____

_____

4. _____

_____

5. _____

_____

Write five *wish* sentences based on the events in the story.

Example: _____ *Mary wishes that she had not missed her flight.*

1. _____

_____

2. _____

_____

3. _____

_____

4. _____

_____

5. _____

_____

B. Choose a completion for each sentence. Write the letter in the space.

    A. he is enjoying himself   D. he had enjoyed himself

    B. he enjoys himself   E. he was enjoying himself

    C. he enjoyed himself

1. Bill is smiling and laughing. He looks as if ___*A*___ .

2. Bill wishes _____ at parties more, but he is too shy to feel comfortable with strangers.

3. If Bill knows most of the people at a party, _____ .

4. Bill looked as though _____ at the holiday party, but he told me later that he had had a terrible time.

5. Bill would go to Mary's next party if _____ at her last one.

6. Tom was laughing and telling jokes all night. He looked as if _____ at the office party.

7. Tom says that _____ at a party if there is plenty to eat and drink.

8. Tom wishes _____ at the wedding, but he was still getting over the flu.

9. If Tom is singing songs and telling jokes, _____ .

10. Tom wishes _____ at his sister's parties, but her friends are all too serious and boring.

11. If _____ , you would have known.

Final Exam

■ PART I

Each of these sentences has only one grammar error.   Find and correct the error.

Example:

chapters
Mary will study a few ~~chapter~~ in her grammar book after she finishes eating her dinner.

1. By the time we found a policeman, the thief had already took my purse and disappeared.

2. As long as some of the job remain unfinished, we will have to keep working.

3. The results of the final exam was posted on the bulletin board outside our professor's office.

4. Every one of the school in our state needs more equipment and school supplies.

5. When none of guests showed up for the party, Mrs. Parker knew that she had forgotten to mail out the invitations.

6. The bad weather created driving conditions that leads to a series of tragic automobile accidents.

7. Even if a person is intelligent, she still needs ambition and little luck in order to get ahead.

8. The president of the company announced that it's employees would not be laid off from their jobs.

9. Although Jack should have won today's competition, he is not discouraging and will try harder next time.

10. Paula must have being very sick yesterday because she usually never misses a chance to go to the movies.

■ PART II

Combine the sentences. Pay attention to the relationship between them. Punctuate carefully.

Example: The police finally found the diamond necklace.
　　　　　 Someone had stolen it in October.

_____ *The police finally found the diamond necklace that had been stolen in October.* _____

1. Mary got an A on her last grammar test.
   John got an A on his last grammar test.

   _____

   _____

2. Susan is watching a TV program.
   The program is discussing the effects of the Internet on society.

   _____

   _____

3. Michael needs to buy a new suit.
   He has an important job interview next Monday.

   _____

   _____

4. First, someone approves your home loan.
   Then, you need to go to the bank to sign some papers.

   _____

   _____

5. "I changed the oil filter in your car."
   The mechanic told Mary this information.

   _____

   _____

6. Barbara can't attend the meeting on Monday.
   Steven can't attend the meeting on Monday.

   _____

   _____

7. The waiter was rude and made a mistake on his bill.
    Robert still goes to that restaurant.

    _____

    _____

8. When will someone complete the new airport?
    No one knows the answer.

    _____

    _____

9. There might be a fire.
    Don't use the elevator to get to the exit.

    _____

    _____

10. The police are trying to find the man.
    Someone found his car near the scene of the crime.

    _____

    _____

11. Susan likes to go shopping on Monday morning.
    The stores are not crowded.

    _____

    _____

12. Barbara wants to go to an island for her vacation.
    The island has warm sandy beaches and lots of sunshine.

    _____

    _____

13. "When are you going to get married and start a family?"
    Tom's mother always asks him this question.

    _____

    _____

14. Mary didn't have enough money.
    She couldn't go skiing with her friends during the winter vacation.

    _____

    _____

15. Roger still has a runny nose and a slight fever.
    He went to work to check his e-mail messages.

    _____

    _____

16. Is John going to marry the woman?
    I met her at the theater last night.

    _____

    _____

17. Wendy needs to take two pills every day.
    Her allergies are very bad in the springtime.

    _____

    _____

18. "I worked at a canning factory for five years."
    Alice told the man this during the job interview.

    _____

    _____

19. Carol's husband is going to take a job in Morocco.
    You met him at my sister's wedding last month.

    _____

    _____

20. Someone killed an old man in a park near her house.
    Mary was shocked.

    _____

    _____

21. First, Barry read many reviews and articles in magazines and newspapers.
Then, he chose a new washing machine and bought it.

_____

_____

22. The carpenter is going to replace the front steps.
Two of the steps have rotten wood.

_____

_____

23. Carolyn decided to take the night job.
She would prefer to work days.

_____

_____

24. Why did Susan cancel their vacation plans?
Peter didn't know the answer.

_____

_____

25. Michael and Theresa have broken their engagement.
That surprises everyone.

_____

_____

Answer Key

CHAPTER 1

■ **Quiz 1** Sample answers
  2. My English class meets at 9 A.M. on Tuesdays and Thursdays.
  3. After I ate dinner last night, I watched TV.
  4. This weekend, I'm going to go to the theater with my parents.
  5. *Shanghai Noon* is playing at a local movie theater.
  6. When I fell asleep last night, I was thinking about my homework for class today.

■ **Quiz 2**
  A.
  1. b. Mary studied her English at 6:00 P.M.
  2. a. John has lived in New York for five years.
     b. Mary has been living in New York for five years.
  3. a. Mary will have eaten dinner before the party begins.
     b. John will eat dinner before the party begins.
  B.
  2. the same
  3. the same

■ **Quiz 3**
  2. asking
  3. preferred
  4. listening
  5. studying
  6. sitting
  7. lying
  8. destroyed
  9. trimmed
  10. opening
  11. training

■ **Chapter 1 Test**
  A.
  1. a. Mary has eaten Italian food.
     b. John ate Italian food last night.
  2. a. John worked in his garden for over an hour.
     b. Mary has been working in her garden for over an hour.
  3. a. John is going to visit his mother next week.
     b. Mary is visiting her mother next week.
  4. a. Mary rides her bicycle for exercise at 7 in the morning.
     b. John is riding his bicycle for exercise.
  5. a. Mary will have finished her homework before she goes to bed.
     b. John will finish his homework before he goes to bed.
  B.
  1. In a, Mary had this experience some time in the past. In b, John did this last night.
  2. In a, John is finished. In b, Mary is still working.
  3. the same
  4. In a, this is Mary's habit. In b, John is doing this at present or right now.
  5. the same

CHAPTER 2

■ **Quiz 1**
  A. Sample answers
  2. A waitress serves customers in a restaurant.
  3. A teacher helps students learn.
  4. A businesswoman works for a business.
  5. A pilot flies an airplane.
  6. A secretary types reports for the boss.
  B. Correct answers use the present progressive.

■ **Quiz 2**
  A.
  2. is tasting
  3. appears
  4. is weighing
  5. seeing
  6. sees
  7. don't feel
  8. surprises
  9. appreciates
  10. is feeling
  B. Sample answers
  2. illogical
  3. polite
  4. unpleasant
  5. noisy
  6. rude
  7. unfair
  8. quiet
  9. lazy
  10. hungry
  11. careless

■ **Quiz 3**
  2. Yes, he laid the papers on the hall table.
  3. Yes, he froze outside today.
  4. Yes, he swam in the 1,000-meter race.
  5. Yes, he lay down for awhile.
  6. Yes, he swept the floor this morning.
  7. Yes, he paid me for the goblet that he broke.

■ **Quiz 4**
  2. began
  3. was working
  4. finished
  5. began
  6. hurt
  7. was riding
  8. made
  9. went
  10. dropped
  11. was shopping

■ **Quiz 5**
  A. Sample answers
  My roommate is constantly using my toothpaste.
  My roommate is forever talking on the telephone.
  My roommate is always borrowing my clothes.
  My roommate is constantly smoking in the bathroom.
  My roommate is forever complaining about how neat I am.

B. Sample answers

2. He was at a night club dancing.
3. He is at the supermarket buying groceries.
4. She is on an airplane flying to Chicago.
5. I was at my grandmother's taking care of her.
6. I'm in the classroom reviewing verb tenses.

■ Chapter 2 Test

A. Sample answers

2. While the woman is walking down the street, she is listening to music.
3. While the young girl was setting the table for dinner, she broke a glass.
4. While the children are doing homework, their father is reading a newspaper and their mother is reading a book.
5. While the young boy was riding his bicycle, he ran into a STOP sign.
6. When the man was picking a flower, a bee stung him on the face.

B. Sample answers

2. is talking to	7. surprised
3. noisy	8. feel
4. lie	9. careless
5. polite	10. bought
6. reading	

CHAPTER 3

■ Quiz 1 Sample answers

2. While Patty was watching TV, her mother told her to come to dinner.
3. Jane has not spoken to Sally since Sally lied to her.
4. Since Susan saw a movie about sharks, she has not swum in the ocean.
5. After Phillip cleaned the wall and fixed the holes, he painted it.
6. Craig broke his arm while he was playing basketball.

■ Quiz 2

2. no change	7. has been living
3. no change	8. has been teaching
4. has been taking	9. no change
5. no change	10. no change
6. has been working	11. has been watching

■ Quiz 3

Michael **began** his college education in 1988. . . . He **graduated** with a degree in English . . . Before he **chose** English as his major, he **had tried** engineering and philosophy. He **decided** to work for a few years before he **went** to graduate school. By the time he **enrolled** . . . he **had gained** valuable experience . . . He **took** four years to finish . . . because he **didn't give** up . . . . Many students **finished** the program in just two years, . . .

■ Quiz 4

2. Correct
3. Correct
4. I have been working since 1990.
5. I had worked as a doctor until I moved to this country.
6. I have never been in a serious earthquake.

■ Chapter 3 Test

B. Sample answers

2. John had been working for ABC Oil Company before he took a job with First National Bank.
3. Karen was working for First National Bank before John joined the bank.
4. Since Karen began to work for the bank, she has dated several men.
5. Since Karen met John, she has not gone out with any other men.
6. John had already been married once before he met Karen.
7. After John and Karen had been dating for a year, John asked Karen to marry him.
8. After John and Karen got married, they looked for an apartment.
9. While John and Karen were looking for an apartment, John lost his job at First National Bank.
10. Since John lost his job, he has gone back to school.
11. Since John got an advanced degree in economics, he has been teaching at the university.

B.

2. Correct
3. Correct
4. Correct
5. After we visited/had visited the big island of Hawaii, we visited Honolulu.
6. Correct
7. Since I stopped smoking, I have gained over thirty pounds from eating candy.
8. Correct
9. Correct
10. After I realized that my math book was gone, I called the campus police.
11. I have never left my books on a library table since I lost my math book.

CHAPTER 4

■ Quiz 1

1. b. I'm going to ask
2. b. I'll get
3. a. Will Ed be OR Is Ed going to be
   b. He'll arrive
4. b. We're going to stay . . . and attend
5. b. I'll meet
6. b. He's going to work
7. b. he'll work
8. b. I'll probably clean

■ Quiz 2

2. As soon as we paint the living room, we'll buy new curtains. OR We'll buy new curtains as soon as we paint the living room.
3. While I'm at the supermarket, I'm going to buy a new dish pan. OR I'm going to buy a new dish pan while I'm at the supermarket.
4. Linda is going to watch TV until her parents tell her to go to bed.
5. Before Mr. Swan teaches a geometry class, he's going to teach an algebra class.
6. As soon as I sweep the kitchen floor, I'm going to mop the kitchen floor.
7. When Bob buys his first car, he's going to give his friends a ride.
8. While Tom finishes/is finishing his law degree, his wife is going to work. OR Tom's wife is going to work while Tom finishes his law degree.
9. After Gary washes the dinner dishes, he's going to read in bed.
10. When the sun comes out, I'm going to go sailing on the lake.
11. After Peter finishes his homework, he's going to see a movie.

■ Quiz 3

A.
2. in the future or habitually
3. in the future
4. in the future
5. now
6. habitually

B.
2. The plane is going to leave at 5:30 P.M.
3. I'm going to/I will arrive in London at noon the next day.
4. I go to Salisbury after I go to London.
5. no change
6. no change

■ Quiz 4

2. I'll be starting/I'm going to be starting a family with my husband.
3. I'll be traveling/I'm going to be traveling in Africa.
4. I'll be taking/I'm going to be taking classes at my local community college.
5. I'll be building/I'm going to be building houses in Ireland.
6. I'll be writing/I'm going to be writing my doctoral thesis.
7. I'll be planning/I'm going to be planning my wedding.
8. I'll be having/I'm going to be having a good time in my retirement.
9. I'll be looking/I'm going to be looking for a new job.
10. I'll be recovering/I'm going to be recovering from eye surgery.
11. I'll be studying/I'm going to be studying engineering at Georgetown University.

■ Quiz 5 Sample answers

2. The European countries will have become one nation.
3. A major earthquake will not have destroyed California.
4. All sea life will not have died from pollution.
5. A single world government will not have been established.
6. The world population will have exceeded 100 billion.
7. People will have been flying to Mars for vacations for many years.
8. A meteor will not have killed all life on earth.
9. Everyone will have been speaking a single language since 2050.
10. People will not have learned to live in peace and love.
11. People will have been living on the moon for 50 years.

■ Chapter 4 Test

A. Sample answers
2. John will have graduated from college before he turns 22 years old.
3. Janice will have been working at the bank for thirty-seven years by the time she retires in November.
4. When Margaret travels in Asia, she is going to visit her sister in Sydney, Australia.
5. While Tony is studying at the library tomorrow night, Peter will be writing his book report at home.
6. The ships will stay in the harbor until the tide comes in.
7. After Michael's airplane leaves tomorrow morning, Karen is going to catch a train for Washington.
8. As soon as Betty picks the ripe apples from her tree, she is going to use them for an apple pie.
9. When Robert grows up and finds a job, he is going to find his own apartment.
10. Mrs. Lee will have gone to bed by the time her daughter comes home from her date.
11. While Amy is cleaning out the garage, her husband will be painting the front door.

B. Sample answers
2. I will have cleaned out my garage. I will have been cleaning the attic gradually.
3. I will have studied all of Chapters 5 and 6. I will have been reviewing Chapters 1 through 4.
4. I will not have exercised at all. I will have been taking swimming lessons for two months.
5. I will have eaten at least ten pizzas. I will have been trying not to eat ice cream.
6. I will have traveled to Birmingham and Manchester. I will have been traveling on the shuttle.

CHAPTER 5

■ Quiz 1 Sample answers

3. As long as Nancy doesn't practice for her interviews, she won't get a job.

4. After Diane read a lot of car magazines, she chose the car that she wanted to buy. OR Diane read a lot of car magazines before she chose the car that she wanted to buy.
5. Since Tim stopped using a dictionary, he has made many spelling mistakes.
6. When Ms. Rodriguez finishes the business report, she will fax a copy to the New York office.
7. While Steven was taking a nap, the earthquake occurred. OR Steven was taking a nap when the earthquake occurred.
8. When Prakash took the bus to work, he got to work an hour early.
9. Whenever Jane is finished reading the newspaper, she puts the newspaper in a bag for recycling.
10. Every time Nina washes the dog, she takes a shower herself.
11. Larry will reread his composition for errors before he turns in his paper.

■ Quiz 2
2. a. was skiing
3. b. ran
4. a. needs
5. b. had been
6. a. has taken
7. c. checks
8. a. will have borrowed
9. b. has rained
10. c. had already eaten
11. a. went

■ Chapter 5 Test
A. Sample answers
2. We will be working on the new project when our boss returns from his vacation.
3. As soon as Joe gets up at 6 A.M., he will do his exercises.
4. Kathy will be living in Texas when her husband returns from his job in South America.
5. After I pick up my cousin at the airport, I'm going to show him the Golden Gate Bridge.
6. Martina is going to go out to dinner with her friends for her birthday before they go dancing at a night club.
7. Maurice was eating lunch in a restaurant when he dropped his napkin on the floor.
8. As soon as Ann gets over her bad cold, she will return to work.
9. After Mary rinses the food off the dishes, she puts the dishes in the dishwasher.
10. By the time Ali's brother gets married, Ali will have graduated from high school.
11. Since the college started offering ESL courses, Becky has been studying ESL.

B.
2. First, Mary flosses and brushes. Then, Mary sees dentist. (present habit)
3. Maybe Mary wins lottery. Then Mary buys cars. (future)
4. First, Mary separates things. Then, Mary puts out the garbage. (future)
5. Mary rides and listens at the same time. (past)
6. First, John watches TV. Then, John does homework. (present habit)

CHAPTER 6
■ Quiz 1
2. needs
3. is
4. doesn't
5. are
6. is
7. require
8. make
9. has
10. leave
11. is

■ Quiz 2
2. Correct
3. Correct
4. incorrect. A lot of my friends recommend . . . .
5. Correct (informal: None of my friends think . . .).
6. incorrect. The number of restaurants in San Francisco exceeds 2,000.
7. incorrect. Each of these bowls is worth more than $150.
8. Correct
9. incorrect. One of my pencils needs . . .
10. incorrect. Half of the airplanes leave on time.
11. incorrect. Every one of the children needs love and affection.

■ Quiz 3 Sample answers
2. There are books in a library. There is a lot of information in a library.
3. There is sand on a beach. There are seashells on a beach.
4. There are packages in a post office. There is mail in a post office.
5. There are pots in a kitchen. There is salt in a kitchen.
6. There are passengers on an airplane. There is luggage on an airplane.

■ Quiz 4
2. come
3. are
4. is
5. have
6. is
7. are
8. is
9. has
10. are
11. is

■ Chapter 6 Test
A. My favorite place **is** a beautiful island called Tranquila. **It is** located 50 miles east of the coast of Florida. The weather on the island **is** very warm all year. There **is** a little rain every afternoon, but each rain storm **lasts** only about 30 minutes. Beautiful white sand beaches **surround** the island. The mountains at the center of the island **are** also wonderful.

The people on Tranquila **are** very friendly to visitors. **They are** happy to give directions to the beach or to the shopping district. Many stores **sell** beautiful jewelry. The jewelry **is** beautiful and cheap, and twenty dollars **buys** a necklace that can cost over a hundred dollars at home. **There are** so many wonderful stores. Make sure you save a lot of time for shopping. Even four hours **is** not enough! If you collect seashells, don't look in the stores. The beaches on Tranquila **are** covered with seashells. You can pick them up for free, so the stores **do not** sell them.

Tranquila is a quiet island. Because **it is** small and far away from other places, **there aren't** any televisions or radios. News **is** available only from one-day-old newspapers from the mainland. **There is** little crime in Tranquila. The police **do not** have much to do except give directions to tourists. Drinking **is** illegal on Tranquila. The number of arrests **is** fewer than three a year. Tranquila has very little pollution, too. **There are** a few cars and trucks, but most people like to walk.

Every visitor **comes** back from Tranquila happy and well rested. All people really **enjoy** the charms of Tranquila and want to visit again soon.

B.
2. Correct
3. incorrect. I don't know how to correct one of the mistakes . . . .
4. incorrect. There is a lot of expensive clothing . . . .
5. Correct
6. Correct
7. incorrect. Is Chinese the most difficult language . . . .
8. incorrect. Studying all night before quizzes is not . . . .
9. incorrect. The flowers in my garden need . . . .
10. Correct
11. incorrect. Growing roses is my neighbor's specialty.

CHAPTER 7

■ Quiz 1
2. feet   6. sheep   9. cacti
3. pianos   7. thieves   10. crises
4. knives   8. mice   11. teeth
5. roofs

■ Quiz 2
A.
2. friend's
3. Doris' or Doris's
4. this morning's
5. men's
6. patients'

B.
2. Taking an afternoon nap.
3. In a bicycle rack.
4. She is a volleyball coach.
5. A four-bedroom house.
6. With a fifteen-dollar check.

■ Quiz 3
Foreston is a former industrial town that is trying to create new jobs and build a healthy *economy*. Foreston is located on a wide river and used to be surrounded by *forests*, which made it an ideal place for the production of *paper* and wood *products*. By 1980, the *hills* around Foreston were empty of *trees*, the factories had closed, and the river was unsafe because of *pollution*. To create new jobs, local *citizens* and city leaders are trying to attract *health* and technology *companies* by offering low *taxes* and cheap *housing*. Local citizens are also concerned about the environment. School groups have cleaned *garbage* out of the river, and the water is safe again for *swimming* and fishing. Every week, volunteers climb the nearby slopes and plant new saplings and scatter wildflower *seeds*. With *patience*, they hope that they will see Foreston surrounded by tall pines, birches, and oaks once again.

■ Quiz 4
1. Last Saturday, I needed to clean my messy office. My desk was covered with **mail**, some scraps of paper, coins, and Ø old magazines. I had old **newspapers** on the floor and old files on a chair. I took **the** mail and threw it away. I sorted **the** scraps of paper and put them in **a** neat stack by the telephone. I put **the change** into my pocket. I looked through **the** old magazines and newspapers, and I decided to put most of them in **the** recycling box. Finally, I put **the** files back in the filing cabinet in their correct places.
2. People collect Ø things for different reasons. Most people hope their collection will increase in value. Many people collect Ø stamps and Ø artwork. My aunt has **an** unusual painting that she bought for ten dollars. It is now worth over two hundred dollars. **Some** people want to remember vacations and trips. Ø Postcards and Ø foreign money are very popular souvenirs. I have **a** friend who collects Ø rocks. He has **a** different story to tell about each rock.

■ Quiz 5
A.
2. many   5. much
3. many   6. many
4. much
B.
2. He had little advice.
3. I had few friends.
4. You need to add little spice (OR few spices) to this soup.
5. You need to spend only a few dollars to get a good camera.
6. This article has little information.

■ Quiz 6
2. Both of the telephones
3. no change
4. Both children and adults
5. no change
6. no change
7. both credit cards and traveler's checks
8. no change
9. both fires
10. Most of the parking spaces
11. no change

■ Quiz 7
3. each of the directions
4. each weekend
5. one of the words/one word

6. Each student
7. Every one of the members
8. One of the problems
9. every light/every one of the lights
10. one of the pills/one pill
11. one of the books

Chapter 7 Test

A.

2. Brian was late to work because there was so much traffic . . . .
3. In our math class, we receive a lot of homework . . . .
4. Every child needs to get shots . . . .
5. John had to wait only a little while . . . .
6. My three-year-old nephew eats only a little rice . . . .
7. Pearl brought too much luggage . . . .
8. Sam wrote each new vocabulary word . . . .
9. The police still do not have much information . . . .
10. Sandra doesn't earn much money . . . .
11. . . . she took few pictures.

B. Last Monday was a holiday, so I didn't have to go to work. I had **many things** to do, and I was happy to have **a little** time to finish all my chores. First I needed to rearrange **some of** the furniture in the living room, which was too crowded. I moved **one of the chairs** from the living room into the **guest bedroom**. I moved another chair into my **son's** room. I put **the** chair in the corner for him to sit and read books in. I moved **the** only sofa in **the** living room against the wall. Now the living room was less crowded.

Next, I needed to clean **some things** in the kitchen. First, I cleaned out **the** refrigerator. I had **lots of** leftover food, and some of it was very old. I threw away **some** rotten tomatoes, **some** old bread, a piece of dried-up chicken, and an open can of soda. I also found **a few** grapes in the back. I didn't know how long they had been there. I wiped off **the** inside of the **vegetable** drawer and the **meat** drawer. Then, I swept and mopped **the** floor. I also scrubbed **the** kitchen sink.

After I had lunch, I did **some** work in my backyard. I mowed the lawn and pulled **a lot of** weeds. I trimmed the branches on **each of my bushes**. I also needed to prune two **rose bushes**. The first one was easy to prune, but **the other** had many thorns. I stuck myself several times. Finally, I planted **some** flowers around **the** front door.

It was 3 P.M. I was exhausted, but very happy. I had finished **all my** chores. My house and my garden looked wonderful. I couldn't wait to see my **family's** faces when they came home from their trip to the zoo.

CHAPTER 8

Quiz 1

2. Yesterday, Susan left **her** purse on the bus when **she** went downtown.
3. Mary got a bad grade on **her** test in Mr. Thomas's class. **She** is going to talk to **him** during **his** office hours tomorrow.
4. Grace and Karl took **their** baby to the doctor for a check-up. **They** need to take **him** in every four months.
5. John doesn't want anybody to touch **his** things, and Julie doesn't want anyone to touch **hers**.
6. **We** are worried that no one will come to our party because no one has called yet.
7. Barbara went to **her** nephew's birthday party yesterday. **She** gave **him** a book that a friend of **hers** had recommended.
8. Teresa bought a sweater as a gift. She is going to give it to **her** brother. She also bought some towels. She is going to give **them** to a friend as a wedding present.
9. If **you** don't finish **your** homework on time, the teacher will ask **you** to correct it by yourself.

Quiz 2

A. Sample answers

2. According to the Hippocratic Oath, a doctor is never supposed to harm his patients. As a result, a doctor has a difficult moral dilemma when a patient asks to be allowed to die.
3. A bus driver has one of the most stressful jobs in a major city. In addition to fighting traffic, a driver needs to deal with angry customers, passengers who try to sneak on without paying a fare, and teenagers who play their music too loud.
4. A zoo can be a very educational place. It gives a person an opportunity to see animals from distant lands. In a zoo, a person might see a hippopotamus, a grizzly bear, a white tiger, and an elephant.
5. A person should see his dentist twice a year. A dentist cleans teeth, but she also checks for diseases and infections that can cause tooth decay and potential problems in the mouth.
6. A computer has become a standard business tool throughout most of the world. It is used to do calculations and word processing, but it is also used for communication and design.

B.

2. it . . . it
3. They want
4. They
5. It . . . includes
6. them . . . are

Quiz 3

2. cut himself
3. enjoyed myself
4. themselves
5. killed himself
6. promised herself
7. didn't stop ourselves
8. talk to myself
9. allowed themselves

10. herself
11. don't take care of yourself

■ Quiz 4

A.

2. specific persons
3. anyone
4. everyone
5. everyone
6. specific person

B.

2. One's memories are all that one has . . . .
3. One should never talk on a cellular phone while driving . . . .
4. If one wants to remember one's dreams, he/she should keep a notebook next to his/her bed and write down all his/her thoughts the moment he/she wakes up.
5. If one runs out of gas on a bridge, there is a $100 fine and a charge for the tow to a gas station.
6. If one doesn't have good health, one can't have a good life.

■ Quiz 5

2. Others
3. another
4. The other
5. the others
6. another, other
7. Other
8. The other
9. others
10. another
11. the other OR the others

■ Quiz 6

2. . . . the two people communicate with each other, help one **another**, and forgive each other.
3. Did I tell you about running into Louis **the other** day?
4. Other than fish, no ~~other~~ pets are allowed in this apartment building.
5. During the war, my mother and father wrote to each **other** every day.
6. no change
7. . . . In **other** words, I can't help you until tomorrow at the earliest.
8. . . . so he will have to see the exhibition of Impressionist paintings on **another** day.
9. . . . It will only take **another** ten minutes.
10. no change
11. . . . I just got one the **other** morning.

■ Chapter 8 Test

A.

1. He	16. it
2. his	17. It
3. they	18. it
4. their	19. They
5. We	20. they
6. our	21. their
7. his/her	22. they
8. He/She	23. themselves
9. his/her	24. it
10. they	25. It
11. they	26. its
12. them	27. it
13. one	28. he/she
14. him/her	29. he/she
15. he/she	30. his/her

B. Sample answers

2. The members of a family should love each other.
3. I can't go to the library today, so I'll have to go another day.
4. Do you know if he has any other friends who can take care of him?
5. The students need another five minutes to finish the test.
6. I visit my grandmother every other week.
7. My washing machine broke down, so I need to buy another one.
8. I would rather pass the class this semester than take it again another time.
9. I prefer to eat chicken than other types of fowl.
10. I'm going to take another chance and buy another lottery ticket.
11. Please talk to one another quietly while I meet with Mr. Brown.

CHAPTER 9

■ Quiz 1 Sample answers

2. Could you please turn down the air conditioning?
3. Would you please put out your cigarette?
4. Could I make an appointment to see you in your office?
5. Could I sit down here?
6. May I leave a message?

■ Quiz 2

2. do we have to
3. must not
4. have to
5. don't have to
6. have to OR must
7. must not
8. have to OR must; had to
9. don't have to
10. don't have to

■ Quiz 3 Sample answers

2. Karen should stop buying things on the Internet. Karen should not have spent so much money.
3. Silvia should have written her thank-you notes right away. She should write them before the new year.
4. Kevin should take care of his own dog. Jane should not care for the dog.
5. Mr. Taylor should have bought the tickets right away. He should apologize to his wife.
6. Marcia should have listened to her mother. Marcia should not have bought the cheap suitcase.

■ Quiz 4 Sample answers

2. You're supposed to wash the cut and stop the bleeding.
3. You're supposed to call the credit card company.
4. You're supposed to turn off the lights and lock the door.
5. You're not supposed to throw the wrapper on the street.

6. You're supposed to wear formal business clothes.
7. You're supposed to return it.
8. You're supposed to give the old man your seat.
9. You're supposed to take a towel and sunscreen.
10. You're supposed to talk to the teacher before class begins.
11. You're supposed to say hello and tell him your name.

■ Quiz 5
2. Why don't we
3. Let's OR We could
4. You could . . . you could
5. Why don't
6. could; Let's OR We could
7. could
8. could
9. Could

■ Chapter 9 Test
A. Sample answers
2. You must listen to the babysitter. OR You must go to bed at 9:00 P.M.
3. Why don't you ask the teacher to let you take the test another day? OR You should go home, and I can tell the teacher you're sick.
4. Jimmy should have gone home and rested. He shouldn't have taken the test.
5. You are supposed to be on time. You are supposed to dress neatly and look professional.
6. When I was working, I had to wake up every morning at 5:30 A.M. I also had to drive through terrible traffic to get to work.
7. Why don't you go to Disneyland? You could go to the Getty Museum.

B.
1. B: have to
   B: could
   A: have to; should; should have
   B: could
   A: Why don't
   A: Why don't we go
   B: could you
   A: had better/have to/should
2. A: Could
   A: have to
   B: should
   B: Why don't you
   A: Could
   B: have to/should . . . had better
   A: have to . . . Could
   B: Would you mind

CHAPTER 10

■ Quiz 1 Sample answers
2. must be
3. must not be
4. might be OR must be
5. would be
6. must be
7. might be
8. must be
9. must be
10. might be OR must be

■ Quiz 2 Sample answers
2. a. She may have left her purse in the cafeteria.
   b. Her purse might be in her counselor's office.
   c. She must have left her purse at home.
3. a. She may have been sick.
   b. The lasagna must have caused the problem.

■ Quiz 3
2. a. Jane
   b. Martha
   c. Mark
3. a. Alice
   b. Kay
   c. Jack
4. a. Ms. Callahan
   b. Mr. Anton
   c. Mrs. Chu

■ Quiz 4 Sample answers
2. might be raining
3. must be leaking
4. should be cleaning up
5. must be meeting OR might be meeting
6. must be looking
7. might be playing . . . might be reading
8. must be studying
9. must be going . . . should be going

■ Quiz 5 Sample answers
2. You can eat popcorn in a movie theater.
3. A bus passenger can read a book.
4. I can drive a car.
5. A cat can climb a tree.
6. You can play computer games.

■ Quiz 6
1. no change
2. no change
3. When my Uncle Stanley was alive, he **would** take us children . . . .
4. no change
5. Every night when my dad got home from work, he **would** sit down . . . .
6. Before Dennis took the spelling improvement class, he **would** always lose . . . .
7. Jake **would** be late for class every morning . . . .
8. no change
9. no change
10. no change
11. no change

■ Quiz 7 Sample answers
2. I would rather have chicken than fish for dinner.
3. I would rather not give you an answer today.
4. I would rather listen to the radio than watch TV right now.
5. I would rather go to the beach than Disneyland on vacation.
6. I would rather do better on the next quiz.
7. I would rather have roses than fruit trees in the backyard.
8. I would rather not cook tonight.
9. I would rather go to New York than San Francisco.

10. I would rather drive than take a taxi.
11. I would rather eat carrots raw than cooked.

■ Chapter 10 Test

A. Sample answers

2. a. may not have been
   b. might have been
   c. must not have been
3. a. may/might be taking
   b. could be taking
   c. must not be taking
   d. must be taking
4. a. must have read
   b. might have read
   c. might not have read

B. Sample answers

2. must be raining . . . should have brought
3. would take . . . would rather go to
4. can leave . . . might be able
5. could drive . . . can't drive
6. must be
7. must have been
8. can change; should be
9. used to tease
10. can't give . . . have to attend
11. would rather have gone . . . must have been

CHAPTER 11

■ Quiz 1

A.

2. The house has been cleaned by the children.
3. Your drink is going to be brought by the waitress very soon.
4. Alex's son is being taken care of by Mary.
5. Many papers are written by the students during the semester.
6. The flower vase in the hall was broken by my little sister.

B.

2. Was the office building damaged by an earthquake?
3. no change
4. More than forty people have been interviewed by Alice for this job.
5. no change (change would be grammatically correct but awkward)
6. no change
7. A solution to the problem is being looked for by the committee.
8. Will our rates be raised by the electric company next month?
9. History has been taught by Barbara for twelve years.
10. no change
11. The East Coast is going to be hit by Hurricane Irene by tomorrow night.

■ Quiz 2

2. The students were greatly pleased by the results of the tests.

3. The report is going to be translated by Jackie from English to Russian.
4. Three packages were left by the mail carrier in my office.
5. no change
6. When was the first personal computer built?
7. The World Cup soccer game on TV is watched by millions of people every year.
8. Several pieces by Bach were performed in the school auditorium last Friday.
9. no change
10. Highway 92 will be finished before winter.
11. A new grammar book is going to be written by Professor Brown during summer vacation.

■ Quiz 3

A.

2. I will be sent the refund within 60 days.
3. The translator will be paid $10 for each page of the document.
4. The businessmen are being shown the new computer chip by Dr. Ikeda.
5. Tom wasn't lent the money for a new car.
6. Ann was taken a casserole by a friend because Ann was sick at home.

B.

2. The refund will be sent to me within 60 days.
3. Ten dollars will be paid to the translator for each page of the document.
4. The new computer chip is being shown by Dr. Ikeda to the businessmen.
5. The money for a new car wasn't lent to Tom.
6. A casserole was taken to Ann by a friend because Ann was sick at home.

■ Quiz 4

2. may have been killed
3. must be checked
4. ought not to be fired
5. has to be finished
6. can't be identified
7. should sit
8. should be split
9. must have been started
10. had better be fixed
11. may be given

■ Quiz 5 Sample answers

2. The person next to me is dressed in red pants and a purple shirt.
3. I am not interested in the football match.
4. One of my friends is terrified of dogs.
5. During the holidays, stores are crowded with shoppers.
6. My classmates are prepared for the next quiz.
7. London is located in southern England.
8. A complete sentence is composed of a subject and a verb.
9. I am excited about my upcoming trip to Canada.
10. All of the students are accustomed to raising their hands in class to ask questions.
11. Are you done with my calculator?

Quiz 6

A.

2. a	5. j	8. f	11. i
3. e	6. k	9. g	
4. h	7. c	10. b	

B.

John:	got sick
John:	am getting better . . . get chilly
John:	got done . . . has gotten busy
Mary:	get rich
John:	get old
Mary:	is getting late . . . get prepared . . . get well
John:	get bored

Quiz 7

2. surprised	7. shocked
3. Correct	8. frustrating
4. excited	9. Correct
5. embarrassing	10. confused
6. Correct	11. Correct

Chapter 11 Test

A. These are the best choices to change:

(2) Schools and many businesses are closed on Thanksgiving Day and the day after.

(6) Stores, homes, and classrooms may be decorated with turkeys, dried leaves, and pumpkins.

(11) The first Thanksgiving Day was held in 1621.

(15) Wild turkeys were easily hunted in the nearby forests.

(16) Thanksgiving was made a legal holiday by Congress in 1941.

These sentences can be changed into the passive, but this shifts the focus away from Thanksgiving.

(3) The beginning of the holiday season is usually marked by Thanksgiving.

(10) Turkey, cranberry sauce, and pumpkin pie are included in a traditional Thanksgiving meal.

B.

2. Michael was hit on the head by a falling pine cone.
3. The machinery is checked five times before it is put in a box for shipping.
4. The weeds on the hill are going to be cut down.
5. The Cancer Foundation was given 2 million dollars by an anonymous donor.
6. All signs and placards should be obeyed.
7. Your car may be towed if you park in this area.
8. The old book was loaned by the museum to the university.

MIDTERM EXAM

1. d	4. a	7. b	10. a
2. b	5. c	8. d	11. b
3. c	6. a	9. c	12. a

13. b	23. d	33. b	42. d
14. a	24. b	34. a	43. a
15. b	25. c	35. d	44. b
16. c	26. a	36. b	45. a
17. c	27. d	37. c	46. d
18. c	28. b	38. c	47. d
19. d	29. d	39. d	48. b
20. a	30. c	40. b	49. a
21. a	31. a	41. c	50. c
22. b	32. d		

CHAPTER 12

Quiz 1

2. The timetable can tell you when Flight 2803 arrives.
3. My little sister wants to know who ate the last piece of pie.
4. Do you know when the next train leaves?
5. I wonder what grade I got on the last quiz.
6. I would like to know how often you go to the gym.
7. Let's ask him what time the meeting starts.
8. Could you tell me which bus goes to the courthouse?
9. Do you know where the nearest mailbox is?
10. I don't know where she went after the meeting.
11. I wonder what color sweater Jim would like.

Quiz 2 Sample answers

2. Do you know if Flight 2803 will arrive on time?
3. My little sister wants to know whether there is any pie left.
4. I wonder if the next train goes to Union City.
5. I would like to know if you are happy with your grade on the last quiz.
6. Can you tell me whether Tom goes to the gym every afternoon?
7. Please tell me whether her meetings usually end on time.
8. Do you know if this bus goes by the courthouse?
9. I'd like to know if the mail has already been picked up.
10. I don't know whether Ruth stayed after school for the meeting.
11. I wonder if Jim would prefer a sweater or a shirt.

Quiz 3 Sample answers

1. to ask
2. to do . . . to begin
3. to stay home
4. to tell you
5. to write . . . to use . . . to hand it in
6. to take the pills
7. to ask

Quiz 4

A.

2. That Sally won't be able to attend the ceremony is unfortunate.

3. It is unlikely that the doctor gave you the wrong prescription.
4. It is a miracle that the little girl survived the plane crash.
5. That Rosa didn't finish the project on time surprises me.
6. That no one will pass this class without additional help from the teacher is clear.

B. Sample answers
2. that I didn't get a higher grade on the test.
3. that I make many grammar mistakes. . . . that I'm too shy to speak.
4. that so many houses were destroyed.
5. that the spelling doesn't follow the pronunciation.

■ Quiz 5

Mr. Thomas told Mary, "You didn't do very well on the last quiz." **He** asked, "**W**hat happened?" and said, "**Y**ou usually do very well on quizzes."

Mary said, "I really didn't have enough time to study. **M**y mother hasn't been well, and I was taking care of her."

"You should have told me," Mr. Thomas remarked. "**Y**ou could have taken the quiz on a different day when you felt more prepared."

"Can I take the quiz again?" asked Mary.

"I'm afraid that you can take a quiz only once," answered Mr. Thomas.

Mary inquired, "**D**o you think that this quiz will lower my grade?"

"Your grades on the first two quizzes were good," he commented, "so your average isn't too bad." **He** added, "**Y**ou can make it up on the next two quizzes."

"I'll do my best," Mary responded. "**T**hanks for talking to me."

■ Quiz 6

Mr. Thomas told Mary that she hadn't done well on the last quiz and asked her **what had happened**. Mary answered **that** she **hadn't had** enough time to study because her mother hadn't been well, and she **had been** taking care of her. Mr. Thomas was surprised and said that she should **have told** him. He explained **that** she could **have taken** the quiz on a different day when she had felt more prepared. Mary wondered **whether** she **could take** the quiz again. Mr. Thomas apologized and told her **that** she **could take** a quiz only once. Mary asked him **if** he thought **that** this quiz **would lower** her grade. Mr. Thomas responded **that** her grades on the first two quizzes were good, so her average **wasn't** too bad. He added **that** she **could** make it up on the next two quizzes. Mary promised **to** do her best and thanked him for talking to her.

■ Quiz 7 Sample answers
2. Janice come to class five minutes early each day.
3. the guests wear formal dress.
4. be on time.
5. make sure that each child had $5 for tickets.

6. they be stored in locked cabinets away from children.
7. pay an admission fee.
8. repaint the outside and inside and remove clutter.
9. tell me in advance.
10. meet again next week.
11. she take some computer courses at the local college.

■ Quiz 8

A.
2. The newspaper will publish whichever drawings win prizes in the school art competition.
3. Wherever he goes, people enjoy talking to him because he has such a friendly and pleasant manner.
4. You get the money for me however you can, as long as you get me the money by the first of the month.
5. The orchestra is ready, and we can start the music whenever you are ready to begin the program.
6. The speaker would be glad to talk to whoever has questions after the lecture.

B.
2. whichever   5. Whoever
3. whatever   6. however
4. whichever

■ Chapter 12 Test

A. Sample answers
2. she turned off the stove before she left the house.
3. he needs to hand in his essay.
4. she should buy her father for his birthday.
5. there is a flight that leaves before noon?
6. she invest in growth stocks.
7. the game will be canceled because of rain.
8. Jim stole his bicycle, but I don't think so.
9. bring his own water and toilet paper.
10. a leaky faucet is fixed?
11. she not be disturbed for the rest of the afternoon.

B.
2. Annie said that her exams had gone well, but that she hadn't had enough time to finish the last question in history class.
3. Robert said that that must have been a tough exam and asked when she would find out her grades.
4. Annie answered that her teachers usually posted them on their office doors on the day after the exam, but she hadn't looked yet.
5. Robert asked what Annie was going to do during the vacation and said that he would be spending the vacation with his uncle in New York.
6. Annie said that she might drive to Los Angeles to visit her cousins, and after that, she didn't know what she was going to do.

CHAPTER 13

■ Quiz 1

2. The red station wagon that caused the accident was driven by a drunk driver.
3. The police talked to the woman whose car had been broken into.
4. The woman that/who/Ø Mr. North just interviewed seemed well qualified for the position.
5. Mrs. Tanaka is looking for the person whose car is blocking her driveway.
6. Joe's parents don't like the music that/which/Ø Joe listens to.
7. My grandmother bought a lot of clothes that/which were on sale.
8. The issue that/which/Ø many people are talking about is not relevant to our current discussion.
9. The printer that/which/Ø Jason bought last week is fast and dependable.
10. People who have advanced computer skills are in great demand in today's job market.
11. The principal presented awards to the children whose artwork was chosen for the citywide art contest.

■ Quiz 2

2. that	7. when/that
3. when	8. where
4. where	9. that
5. that	10. that
6. that	11. when/that

■ Quiz 3 Sample answers

2. who has free time
3. that I can bring
4. who can bag groceries
5. that are smaller . . . that are larger
6. that contains sugar
7. that I want
8. that I've forgotten
9. that has four-wheel drive
10. who wants a copy of my speech

■ Quiz 4

A.

2. no change
3. no change
4. I have looked everywhere for my grammar book, which I am sure I left on the dining table.
5. Paul will call you at 5:30 P.M., when he will be home from work.
6. no change
7. The roof of my house, which is already 20 years old, is leaking and badly in need of repair.
8. no change
9. The Red Cross, which provides humanitarian aid to victims of wars and natural disasters, is the favorite charity of the president's wife.
10. I recently got the autograph of J.K. Rowling, who is the author of the Harry Potter series of books.
11. no change

B.

2. a	4. a	6. a
3. a	5. b	

■ Quiz 5

A.

2. Mrs. White won first prize for her apple pie, the crust of which was exceptionally light and flaky.
3. When Craig got a new job in California, his wife had to find a new job and his children had to change schools, which was a very difficult situation for everyone.
4. The repairs to Jane's car were finished the same day, which she was very pleased about.
5. Mr. Carter talked to a large group of college students, many of whom did not know that he used to be the president.
6. The workers, most of whose jobs were in danger because of consolidation and cost-cutting, attended the meeting about the merger of the two companies.

B.

2. the noun (bus)
3. the noun (assignment)
4. the sentence
5. the noun (Dalian)
6. the sentence

■ Quiz 6

2. The books Alex needs for his research paper are available only at the main library.
3. The contestant answering all ten questions correctly in less than one minute will win $64,000.
4. Pam is taking the train leaving for Budapest at 9:08 P.M.
5. This marble statue, sculpted by Bernini in 1678, is expected to sell for more than a million dollars at auction.
6. no change
7. no change
8. My father is looking for a recliner covered in dark brown leather.
9. Firemen are quite concerned because the hills surrounding the city are very dry and could easily catch fire.
10. You need to speak to the woman talking on the telephone.
11. Children having dirty hands must wash them before they can eat dinner.

■ Chapter 13 Test

A. Sample answers

2. The shirt that John spilled wine on has to be cleaned.
3. Mary needs to talk to the neighbor whose dog dug a big hole in her flower bed.
4. The bus John takes in the morning is crowded.
5. John and Mary decided to hire the woman who had three years of experience.
6. The flowers that are in the front yard look wonderful.

7. The people who wanted to smoke had to go outside.
8. Their boss is trying to find a time when both John and Mary are free.
9. Mary is going to go to the store that is two blocks from her house.
10. Mary is going to wear the suit that her mother gave her to her interview.
11. The street that is behind John's house usually has some parking.

B.
2. After working out in the weight room for 35 minutes, John took a quick shower and then soaked in the Jacuzzi, which felt very good.
3. Mr. Frank Brown, a well-known authority on World War I, is going to give a lecture at the Civic Auditorium.
4. Tim is going to throw away his old suitcase, which has a broken wheel.
5. The interview committee read the resumes of over 200 applicants, only ten of whom would be chosen for in-person interviews.
6. The temperature in the Northeast was above 100 degrees for a week, which caused the deaths of several elderly people and young children.

CHAPTER 14

■ Quiz 1 Sample answers
2. Mrs. Grant is devoted to helping the homeless.
3. Larry is thinking of going to the Caribbean for his vacation.
4. My baby shows me she is hungry by crying.
5. Sarah is not used to wearing short pants in the winter.
6. Our class is responsible for cleaning up the lower yard.
7. Everyone is looking forward to having a three-day weekend.
8. All of the students are worried about passing the final exam.
9. Fred fixed his broken eyeglasses by using some glue.
10. Are you interested in coming to a lecture on the rain forest?
11. Do you really think that Sonya is guilty of selling secret documents?

■ Quiz 2 Sample answers
2. I caught my little sister listening at my bedroom door.
3. Mike likes to go hiking in the hills near his home.
4. Maria spent two hours choosing a dress for the party.
5. The old men sit on the park bench watching the passers-by.
6. Craig hates to go shopping on the weekend.
7. I had a hard time learning all of the irregular verbs.
8. I waste a lot of time looking for my keys every morning.

9. We all had fun visiting you and your family.
10. Barbara and Jack couldn't stand waiting in line for an hour for the store to open.
11. Mrs. Smith found her neighbor's dog digging in her flower bed.

■ Quiz 3 Sample answers
2. playing
3. to spend
4. jogging
5. to call
6. to stay
7. to host
8. to turn down
9. to have
10. planting
11. to keep
12. to wear
13. to speak
14. to go
15. smelling

■ Quiz 4 Sample answers
A.
2. It takes a long time to write a book.
3. It should not be hard to fix your glasses.
4. It might be boring to attend the lecture.
5. It cost a lot of money for us to go to Australia.
6. It is unusual to see seals at this time of year.

B.
2. Writing a book takes a long time.
3. Fixing your glasses should not be hard.
4. Attending the lecture might be boring.
5. Going to Australia cost us a lot of money.
6. Seeing seals at this time of year is unusual.

■ Chapter 14 Test Sample answers
2. of staying
3. for borrowing
4. reviewing; to get
5. bringing
6. Giving
7. to be checked
8. to be late for
9. standing; to go
10. sneezing
11. at cooking . . . to hire
12. in learning . . . to visit
13. skiing
14. to buy . . . looking . . . and doing
15. taking . . . to be determined
16. with watching . . . to read
17. to read . . . to be
18. by thawing
19. Taking care of; to relax
20. lying

CHAPTER 15

■ Quiz 1 Sample answers
2. in order to ride on an historic train.
3. in order to take pictures in Banff.
4. in order to meet her boyfriend in Toronto at the end of the trip.
5. in order to meet Pauline.

Quiz 2 Sample answers

2. A person is ready to get married when he is ready to settle down.
3. A student who does not study or review is apt to fail a course.
4. I am willing to parachute out of an airplane.
5. I am certain to go to London next year.
6. One should be prepared to escape from the house.
7. I have been lucky to find a twenty-dollar bill in a gym locker.
8. Most people are reluctant to go to the dentist.
9. I was surprised to discover how easy English is to learn.
10. I am determined to swim off the Great Barrier Reef in Australia.
11. I am always careful to spell correctly on my papers.

Quiz 3

1. too heavy
2. too sick (I am not well enough to go to work.)
3. tall enough (She is too short.)
4. too slowly (You aren't driving fast enough.)
5. hot enough (It is still too cold.)
6. carefully enough (You are too careless.)

Quiz 4

1. to be washed
2. to be revised; to hand
3. to be cooked; to start
4. to be thrown
5. to fill out; to be filled out
6. to answer
7. to be sold

Quiz 5

2. You should take advantage of their selling phone service for 50 percent off.
3. I'm sure that Mr. Grant will apologize for his children breaking your kitchen window with a baseball.
4. Fatima's husband has been complaining about her going shopping every weekend and spending a lot of money.
5. Although I love having houseguests, I am looking forward to their leaving soon.
6. Mr. Wah's divorcing his wife after 23 years stunned everyone.
7. Mark was very proud of his mother's returning to school to finish her college education.
8. Martha is always afraid of her husband's not being dressed before their dinner guests arrive.
9. The manager resented his employee talking to the vice-president before talking to him.
10. I can't stand their always complaining but never doing anything to help improve the situation.
11. Matthew is prepared for his opponent's trying to steal the ball from him.

Quiz 6 Sample answers

2. burning
3. flying
4. rubbing
5. smoking
6. crying
7. walking
8. beeping
9. shaping
10. shaking
11. exploding

Quiz 7 Sample answers

2. help me lift heavy things.
3. understand the directions?
4. to dance with her.
5. put them back.
6. find your way.
7. use our books during the quiz?
8. to start.
9. run around the field two times.
10. late for the party.
11. take a break for ten minutes.

Chapter 15 Test

A. Sample answers

2. I was shocked to get a "D" on my last quiz.
3. I am determined to get a better grade next time.
4. I was too tired to finish my essay last night.
5. I don't have enough time to go to the library to study.
6. I need to plan my trip to Washington, D.C.
7. I am considering buying a new suitcase for my trip.
8. I heard some people talking about how beautiful it is in Canada.
9. Corinne helped by finding the word in her dictionary.
10. I have to call my travel agent this afternoon.
11. I stopped reading my textbook at midnight.

B.

2. Our house needs to **be repaired** and **painted** before we can consider ~~to selling~~ it.
3. There isn't enough time ~~to~~ **for** us ~~for finishing~~ **to finish** all of the reports by Friday.
4. Sally was sorry to have ~~being~~ **been** late, and she apologized ~~to have~~ **for having** missed part of the presentation.
5. Jason has been thinking about ~~he~~ moving out of the house and ~~find~~ **finding** a job.
6. I heard the rain ~~fell~~ **falling** on the roof and realized that I needed ~~bringing~~ **to bring** an umbrella with me.
7. My doctor made me ~~to~~ **wait** 45 minutes before he would see me.
8. Mrs. Won wouldn't let her son ~~played~~ **play** football because she was worried about ~~he gets~~ **his getting** hurt.
9. These jeans are ~~tight enough~~ **too tight** for me to wear anymore.
10. The president had the company ~~putting~~ **put** off sending out its annual report.
11. We all look forward to ~~you will give~~ **your giving** the valedictory speech at graduation.

CHAPTER 16

■ Quiz 1

2. The new magazine was colorful and glossy and had lots of photographs and advertising.
3. The fireman put out a fire, rescued a cat stuck in a tree, and helped a man who had had a heart attack.
4. In Brazil, I saw white sand beaches, beautiful young women and men, and crystal clear blue water.
5. When Jane got home from work, she took off her suit and high-heeled shoes and put on an old pair of jeans, an old pair of slippers, and a warm wool sweater.
6. For dinner, Kevin ate slices of roast beef, rice with gravy, and string beans and drank a glass of wine.

■ Quiz 2

2. Either Cindy or Mrs. Smith will babysit the kids this evening.
3. During the holiday weekend, the parking lots at both San Francisco International Airport and San Jose Airport were full.
4. Both bread and flour should be stored in the freezer instead of the refrigerator.
5. Neither Arthur nor his cousins have ever been to Disneyland.
6. The earthquake both knocked over several freeways and broke gas and water lines.
7. Philip wants neither to go to college nor to find a job.
8. The contractor will either try to repair the broken fence or tear down the fence and replace it.
9. Both oranges and cabbage are good sources of vitamin C.
10. Neither mayoral candidate Jim Brown nor mayoral candidate Alicia Taylor talked about the homeless problem.
11. The severe rain storm both flooded basements and sewers and caused mudslides.

■ Quiz 3

2. Polly was looking for a new camera for her brother's birthday. She wanted a large selection and good prices, so she used the Internet to do her shopping.
3. Both Silvia and her husband love the rock band The Rolling Stones, but they refuse to pay $80 a ticket to attend a concert.
4. no change
5. Acme Toy Company continues to produce dolls, metal cars, construction sets, and action figures, but it no longer makes bicycles or board games.
6. Flights 2058 and 2065 to Los Angeles have been delayed, but Flight 2061 is departing on time. I can get you a seat on Flight 2061.
7. I have tried the pineapple diet. I have tried the starch diet and the protein diet, too, but none of them worked.
8. The weather forecaster predicts heavy fog and light drizzle in the morning, but clear skies and sunshine for the late afternoon.
9. Mary doesn't like to drink tea or decaffeinated coffee, so we need to pick up some regular coffee for her.
10. Bicycles, motorcycles, and handicapped drivers can park in Lot A, but everyone else needs to park in Lots B or C.
11. Barbara has had many different jobs. She has been a flight attendant, a sales clerk, a waitress, and a receptionist, but now she has her MBA and is the regional manager for a large multinational corporation.

■ Chapter 16 Test

2. Linda has traveled by car, bus, and train, but she has not traveled by ship, plane, or balloon.
3. Thomas has read about computers and the Internet, and he has taken classes in computer programming and applications.
4. At her surprise birthday party, Gloria was surprised to see her high school friends, her aunt and uncle from New York City, and her old college roommate, but she was disappointed not to see her sister or her niece.
5. Last winter, Cincinnati experienced terrible storms and flooding, unending rain, and devastating tornadoes and hail.
6. Next weekend, Shirley may visit her grandmother or her sister, do some shopping, or take in a movie, but she has to do the laundry and clean the bathroom.
7. Both Anita and Sandra love to play volleyball, but neither Betty nor Jackie likes sports.
8. Last night, Larry watched some TV, surfed on the Internet, listened to some music, and read the newspaper, but today he has to do some serious work.
9. Mr. Kincaid owns real estate, stocks, and bonds, but he has to sell some stocks and bonds to pay his taxes.
10. Both Craig and Jean have good computer skills and can type 70 words a minute, so they both got jobs as executive secretaries.
11. Both French and German are Indo-European languages, but neither Chinese nor Korean is an Indo-European language.
12. It was an extremely cold day, so Mark put on a heavy sweater and a warm jacket, but he didn't wear a hat or a scarf.
13. This apartment has no air conditioning, no closet space, a broken stove, and peeling paint, so I really need to find a new apartment.
14. When Steve had his skiing accident, he broke two ribs, his collar bone, his wrist, and his arm, but he didn't sustain any head or spinal injury.
15. I can sleep on the couch or on the floor, so you don't have to be so polite and give me your bed.
16. This magazine has interesting articles about Hawaii, mountain climbing, and different cultural customs, and useful articles about getting the best airfares and the best times of year to travel.

CHAPTER 17

■ Quiz 1 Sample answers

2. Because John arrived at the airport just 10 minutes before his flight was scheduled to depart, he nearly missed his plane.
3. Now that the rain has stopped, we can open the windows and get some fresh air.
4. We will have to contact Mr. Adams by mail since he has neither e-mail nor fax.
5. Sue did not enjoy going to the movies because she had left her eyeglasses at home.
6. Larry has to do a lot of traveling now that he is the senior manager for the western division of his company.
7. We can stay up late and talk since we don't have to go to work tomorrow.
8. I need to find a new place to get my hair cut now that my barber has retired after 25 years.
9. Because the two groups refused to sign the peace treaty, fighting between them has begun again.
10. Future funding for the space program is uncertain since the last three space missions failed.
11. Because cigarette taxes have risen, the price of cigarettes has risen 400 percent in the last three years.

■ Quiz 2

2. e	5. i	8. c	11. a
3. f	6. h	9. d	
4. j	7. g	10. k	

■ Quiz 3 Sample answers

2. If you forget to set your alarm clock, you may oversleep. If you get in late at night, you might forget to set your alarm clock.
3. If the price of gasoline goes up, it will be more expensive to go on vacation. If the price of gasoline goes up, air fares will rise as well.
4. If your boss doesn't give you a raise, you should look for another job. If you keep getting to work late, your boss might not give you a raise.
5. If the police stop Larry for driving above the speed limit, he will get an expensive ticket. If Larry gets a ticket, his insurance rate will probably go up.
6. If you need to talk with me tomorrow, call me at the office. If you need to talk to me tomorrow, call me in the morning.

■ Quiz 4 Sample answers

2. there is more work to do.
3. , here are our cell phone and pager numbers.
4. , stay calm and protect your head.
5. the sun comes out.
6. , he will still pass the class.

■ Quiz 5

2. only if	5. Only if	8. only if	11. only if
3. Only if	6. Only if	9. Unless	
4. unless	7. only if	10. unless	

■ Chapter 17 Test

A. Sample answers

2. , we will have to cancel the hike.
3. , you should make your best guess.
4. her car is in the shop.
5. , you will need to undergo chemotherapy.
6. you have other things to do.
7. others do not.
8. , you must not leave the scene of the accident until the police arrive.
9. I promise to drive carefully.
10. it was too cold this winter.
11. should you interrupt the meeting.

B.

2. If	9. Unless
3. Even though	10. Even though
4. Unless	11. If
5. if	12. even though
6. because	. . . because
7. Even though	13. if
. . . because	14. Unless
8. unless	

CHAPTER 18

■ Quiz 1

2. No change
3. Before throwing anything away, Mary consulted with John to make sure it was okay.
4. Since moving into their house in 1992, Mary and John have acquired a lot of furniture.
5. While on vacation in Venice, Italy, the Wilsons bought a lot of glass sculpture.
6. Before leaving Italy, the Wilsons had all the sculpture sent to their home in the United States.
7. No change
8. Since taking their trip to Italy, the Wilsons have been collecting glass from all over the world.
9. No change
10. While searching for information, Joe's sister found two other cars that she thought would interest him.
11. After reading all the articles that his sister had found for him, Joe chose which car he wanted.

■ Quiz 2

A.

2. (While) Delivering newspapers on his bicycle, Pete was attacked by a large, ferocious dog.
3. Not (being) able to manage her time well, Sally was late with all of her class assignments.
4. Working 14 hours a day at two different jobs, Mike does little more than sleep when he gets home.
5. (While) Studying for his grammar test in the library, Jack fell asleep.
6. Not having enough time to clean her house, Clare has a housecleaner who comes every other week.

B.

2. while	5. because
3. while	6. because OR while
4. because	

■ Quiz 3

2. Upon being elected mayor of the city, Jane Peters set up a committee to study the public schools.
3. Upon returning from a trip to Mexico, Mrs. Alexander started a small business that sold Mexican handicrafts.
4. Upon having had her sixth baby, Tina said, "I think this will be my last one."
5. Upon finishing her final exam, Minal breathed a sigh of relief.
6. Upon finding a gold coin in the sand at the beach, Tom couldn't believe his good luck.

■ Chapter 18 Test

A.
2. While Joe was lying in bed and feeling depressed, he wondered what he would do now that he no longer had a job.
3. Because Johnny had no money to buy a present for his mother, he made her a birthday card.
4. After the research scientists test the drug on mice, they will test the drug on monkeys.
5. Since Alex took a course in public speaking, he has developed more self-confidence.
6. When Jane arrives in London, the first thing she will do is have tea at the Ritz Hotel.
7. Because Carol was confused about the directions to the party, she had to stop at a gas station to ask for help.
8. Before Brian left for India, he had to get several shots to protect him from tropical diseases.
9. While Omar was talking with his accountant, he realized that starting his own business would be quite complicated.
10. When Chef Louis tasted Mrs. Wilson's blueberry pie, he declared that it was the most delicious pie he had ever eaten.
11. While Susan was working in her garden, she disturbed a wasp's nest and was stung several times.

B.
2. After explaining the medical procedure, the doctor asked the patient if he had any questions.
3. While George was standing on a ladder to change a light bulb, his dog ran by and knocked the ladder over.
4. Since reading a book about sharks, Sam has been afraid to swim in the ocean.
5. When it began to rain, Luisa opened her umbrella.
6. (While) Playing basketball with his friends, my brother fell and sprained his ankle.
7. After finishing his homework assignment, Paul was free to watch TV for the rest of the evening.
8. After becoming a citizen, the first thing Mr. Santos did was register to vote.
9. Having no husband and three children, Mrs. Nguyen had to work ten hours a day to keep them fed and clothed.
10. Not having received a package from her brother, Jane contacted the post office about tracking the package.

11. Since graduating from the university with a degree in French History, George has been looking for a position at a university.

CHAPTER 19

■ Quiz 1

2. a. Mary had to retake the Introduction to Physics class because she got a failing grade.
   b. Mary had to retake the Introduction to Physics class because of her failing grade.
3. a. The minister of finance raised the interest rates because he was afraid of inflation.
   b. The minister of finance raised the interest rates because of his fear of inflation.
4. a. Although Bill wanted to study art, he majored in engineering because his father pressured him to do so.
   b. Although Bill wanted to study art, he majored in engineering because of pressure from his father.
5. a. During the hot summer, ants come inside homes because they are searching for water.
   b. During the hot summer, ants come inside homes because of their search for water.
6. a. The space ship to Mars got lost because scientists had made errors in their calculations.
   b. Due to errors in the scientists' calculations, the space ship to Mars got lost.

■ Quiz 2

2. There were large crowds at the mall, so Sally did her shopping over the Internet.
3. Ron was fired from his job because he was late to work for the third time.
4. Fewer people are saving money in banks because of the 40 percent rise in the stock market over the last year.
5. It is easier to get admitted to a college in the United States, so many students come here.
6. The movie is no longer showing in the theater. Therefore, we will have to wait until it comes out on video.
7. Bill can't lift heavy objects because he injured his lower back.
8. Larry heard that his friend was in the hospital. Consequently, he sent him a card and some flowers.
9. Due to a snag in the sweater Jane bought, she needs to return it to the store and exchange it.
10. The extension to the subway line will not open on time because there have been many construction delays.
11. The previous owners never took care of their house, so it is now quite dilapidated.

■ Quiz 3 Sample answers

2. unemployment is at a record low.
3. no one believes anything he says.
4. their tusks can be sold for ivory.

5. teachers ask her to help other students with their work.
6. he won't make a mistake in spelling.
7. they have no shelter from the weather.
8. he had to borrow money from the bank.
9. he doesn't even know how to print.
10. he could access the Internet.
11. I couldn't put it down.

■ Quiz 4

2. **Nevertheless,** it is still not running smoothly.
3. **Because** Thomas left his reading glasses at home, he wasn't able to read the menu.
4. Howard is a careful driver, **so** he never gets a traffic ticket.
5. **Even though** Emily skipped breakfast, she still has a lot of energy.
6. Fewer people in the Bay Area can afford to buy a house **because of** the sharp increase in home prices in the last six months.
7. Mr. Kwan is a rich man, **but** he still refuses to buy his daughter a new car.
8. **Despite** his busy schedule, Ali still found time to coach his son's baseball team.
9. Mark collects old fountain pens, **so** he loves to visit antique stores wherever he goes.
10. **Even though** Martina fell in the ice skating competition, the judges still gave her high scores.
11. . . . **even though** the postage was quite high.
12. Tarek is very afraid of dogs **because** he was bitten by one as a child.
13. **Because of** the favorable exchange rate, many people are going to Canada for vacations.
14. **Even though** the freeway has been widened to five lanes, the traffic is still terrible.
15. Anne really loves to eat mangoes, **but** she refuses to pay $2.00 for one.
16. Brian's office is going to get a new copier **despite** the fact that the old one works fine.

■ Quiz 5 Sample answers

2. Uncle Philip is very knowledgeable, but Aunt Margaret gives the best advice.
3. Uncle Philip has gotten rather fat. However, Aunt Margaret has remained very slender.
4. Uncle Philip has a very loud voice, whereas Aunt Margaret is very soft-spoken.
5. Uncle Philip is a self-made man. On the other hand, Aunt Margaret comes from a very well-to-do background.
6. While Uncle Philip only pretends to be gruff and stern, Aunt Margaret is really quite strict.

■ Quiz 6 Sample answers

2. I have to get home by 10 P.M., or else my dad will punish me.
3. The government should plan for the increasing number of retired people. Otherwise, there will be no money in the social security system in the future.
4. People must voluntarily obey the laws, or else there will be chaos.

5. Access to the Internet must be available to all people. Otherwise, the right to freedom of speech is endangered.
6. You should mail in your application right away, or else you might lose your chance for that job.

■ Chapter 19 Test

A. Sample answers
2. I didn't wear a jacket because I wasn't cold.
3. I need to wear a jacket. Otherwise, I will be cold.
4. It was cold outside, but I didn't wear a jacket.
5. It was a warm day, so I didn't wear a jacket.
6. I didn't wear a jacket despite the cold.
7. It was a cold day. Consequently, I wore a jacket.
8. Due to the cold weather, I wore a jacket.
9. It was such a cold day that I wore a jacket.
10. I had better wear a jacket, or else I will be cold.
11. It was a cold day. However, I didn't wear a jacket.
12. Unless I wear a jacket, I'll be cold.
13. If it isn't warm outside, I'll wear a jacket.
14. It is a warm day. Nevertheless, I'm going to wear a jacket.
15. It was quite warm yesterday, whereas it's quite cold today.

B. Sample answers
2. . . . I drank four glasses of water.
3. . . . tree, it didn't produce any apples.
4. . . . treatment, people are living longer and healthier lives.
5. . . . people talk too loud in small spaces such as restaurants and buses.
6. . . . the economy will improve.
7. . . . car, she will have to take the bus.
8. . . . crop. Therefore, the price of oranges will be much higher this summer.
9. . . . year, she wants to go there again.
10. . . . smoking, or else he may suffer a heart attack.
11. . . . he is a very nice guy.

CHAPTER 20

■ Quiz 1 Sample answers

2. If Mary goes to Paris for vacation, she will not go to London.
3. If Geoffrey loses his job, he will have a hard time finding another one.
4. If Larry doesn't have enough money for a new car, he will have to buy a used one.
5. If the price of gasoline goes up, cars will need to get better gas mileage per gallon.
6. If there isn't enough time to finish Chapter 20, you will have to study it on your own.

■ Quiz 2 Sample answers

2. If I were ten years older, I would not feel much different.
3. If I could speak and write English fluently, I wouldn't have to take ESL courses.

4. If I could predict the future, I would not tell anybody else.
5. If I could fly, I would take amazing pictures from the air.
6. If I were a famous movie star, I would have a private language tutor.

■ Quiz 3

2. If Karen had invested money in the stock market last year, she would have made a lot of money.
3. If Paula hadn't twisted her ankle, she could have finished the marathon.
4. If Michael hadn't gotten three traffic tickets last year, his insurance rates wouldn't have gone up.
5. If John had wanted to move to South Dakota, he would have accepted the job offer.
6. If George had worn a jacket or a sweater, he wouldn't have caught a bad cold.
7. If Mr. Martinez hadn't tried to move the heavy sofa by himself, he wouldn't have pulled a muscle in his lower back.
8. If Linda's grandchildren hadn't come to visit her, she would have visited them.
9. If Sally Smith had gotten 260 more votes, she would have been elected mayor.
10. If Alex had put the ice cream in the freezer, it wouldn't have melted.
11. If Susie had practiced the piano, she would have been able to play her pieces for her lesson.

■ Quiz 4

Paul is paying his monthly bills. He is very worried because there are a lot of bills. If he hadn't spent so much money, he wouldn't be so worried right now. What if he doesn't have enough money?

He looks at the bills one by one. The first one is for repairs to his car. If he **hadn't sent** his car to the garage for repairs, he **would have saved** $600. However, if he **hadn't had** a car to drive for the last month, he **wouldn't have been able to** go to work and he **wouldn't be able to** pay any bills right now.

The second bill is for the rent. If he doesn't pay his rent, he **will have** no place to live, so he has to pay this bill. The next bill is for his dentist. Paul developed a serious toothache three weeks ago. If he **hadn't gone** to the dentist right away, his tooth **would be giving** him problems.

The fourth bill is for repairs to his television. When Paul bought his television, he decided not to get an extended warranty. If he **had gotten** it then, it **would have cost** only $79 extra. Instead, he had to pay over $150 for the repairs because the warranty has expired.

The fifth bill is for the department store. Paul bought four new shirts and three pairs of pants. The bill is for $450. If he **had bought** only one shirt and one pair of pants, he **would owe** only $125.

Paul can't believe how much money he spent over the past month. If he **had kept** track of his spending, he probably **wouldn't be** in this situation. After he pays his bills, if he **doesn't have** enough money to live on, he will have to take money out of savings.

■ Quiz 5

A.

2. Had the authorities been more vigilant, the disaster could have been avoided.
3. Should there be more problems with your furnace, call this phone number.
4. Had the residents received the warning earlier, fewer people would have been killed in the tornado.
5. Were I sixteen again, I would try to enjoy my youth more.
6. Should you have any problems with your purchase, you can bring it back for a complete refund.

B. Sample answers

2. I would have given you a ride, but I didn't have a car.
3. Mary would have passed the test, but she didn't have enough time to study.
4. Mary would like to go shopping with us, but she has to pick her kids up from school.
5. The government would build more public housing, but it doesn't have enough money.
6. The government would eliminate poverty, but it doesn't know how to.

■ Quiz 6 Sample answers

2. I feel as if I could sleep ten hours.
3. It looks as if a tornado had been through here.
4. You sound as if you are coming down with a cold.
5. It looks as though she got stuck in traffic.
6. It smells as if some of the food has spoiled.

■ Quiz 7

2. did	10. did
3. didn't	11. couldn't
4. were	12. weren't
5. could have	13. were
6. did	14. could
7. were	15. weren't
8. hadn't	16. hadn't
9. had	

■ Chapter 20 Test

A. Sample answers

1. If Mary had confirmed her taxi reservation, her taxi would have come on time.
2. If there hadn't been an accident on the freeway, she would probably have made her flight.
3. If she hadn't left her purse at home, she would have made her flight.
4. If the taxi company hadn't lost her reservation, the taxi would have come on time.
5. If Mary hadn't had her house keys in the suitcase pocket, she could not have gotten her purse.

1. Mary wishes that she had confirmed her taxi reservation.
2. Mary wishes that the taxi company hadn't lost her reservation.
3. Mary wishes that there hadn't been an accident on the freeway.

4. Mary wishes that she hadn't left her purse at home.
5. Mary wishes that she had taken the train.

B.

2. C   5. D   8. D   10. C
3. B   6. E   9. A   11. D
4. E   7. B

FINAL EXAM
Part I

1. By the time we found a policeman, the thief had already ~~took~~ **taken** my purse and disappeared.
2. As long as some of the job ~~remain~~ **remains** unfinished, we will have to keep working.
3. The results of the final exam ~~was~~ **were** posted on the bulletin board outside our professor's office.
4. Every one of the ~~school~~ **schools** in our state needs more equipment and school supplies.
5. When none of **the** guests showed up for the party, Mrs. Parker knew that she had forgotten to mail out the invitations.
6. The bad weather created driving conditions that ~~leads~~ **led** to a series of tragic automobile accidents.
7. Even if a person is intelligent, she still needs ambition and **a** little luck in order to get ahead.
8. The president of the company announced that ~~it's~~ **its** employees would not be laid off from their jobs.
9. Although Jack should have won today's competition, he is not ~~discouraging~~ **discouraged** and will try harder next time.
10. Paula must have ~~being~~ **been** very sick yesterday because she usually never misses a chance to go to the movies.

Part II Sample answers

1. Both Mary and John got an A on their last grammar test.
2. Susan is watching a TV program that (OR which) discusses the effects of the Internet on society.
3. Michael needs to buy a new suit because he has an important job interview next Monday.
4. After your home loan is approved, you need to go to the bank to sign some papers.
5. The mechanic told Mary that he had changed the oil filter in her car.

6. Neither Barbara nor Steven can attend the meeting on Monday.
7. Even though the waiter was rude and made a mistake on his bill, Robert still goes to that restaurant.
8. No one knows when the new airport will be completed.
9. If there is a fire, don't use the elevator to get to the exit.
10. The police are trying to find the man whose car was found near the scene of the crime.
11. Susan likes to go shopping on Monday morning because the stores are not crowded.
12. Barbara wants to go to an island for her vacation that has warm sandy beaches and lots of sunshine.
13. Tom's mother always asks him when he is going to get married and start a family.
14. Mary didn't have enough money, so she couldn't go skiing with her friends during the winter vacation.
15. Even though Roger still has a runny nose and a slight fever, he went to work to check his e-mail messages.
16. Is John going to marry the woman I met at the theater last night?
17. Because Wendy's allergies are very bad in the springtime, she needs to take two pills every day.
18. Alice told the man during the job interview that she had worked at a canning factory for five years.
19. Carol's husband, whom (OR who) you met at my sister's wedding last month, is going to take a job in Morocco.
20. Mary was shocked that an old man was killed in a park near her house.
21. After reading many reviews and articles in magazines and newspapers, Barry chose a new washing machine and bought it.
22. The carpenter is going to replace the front steps, two of which have rotten wood.
23. Carolyn decided to take the night job although she would prefer to work days.
24. Peter didn't know why Susan canceled their vacation plans.
25. It surprises everyone that Michael and Theresa have broken their engagement.